China Today

Published in association with
Observer Research Foundation
New Delhi

Observer Research Foundation (ORF) is a public policy think-tank that aims to influence formulation of policies for building a strong and prosperous India. The ORF pursues these goals by providing informed and productive inputs, in-depth research and stimulating discussion. The Foundation is supported in its mission by a cross-section of India's leading public figures, academics and business leaders.

China Today

Politics, Society & Culture

ORF CHINA STUDIES SERIES # 1

ACADEMIC FOUNDATION
NEW DELHI

www.academicfoundation.com

First published in 2011
by

ACADEMIC FOUNDATION
4772-73 / 23 Bharat Ram Road, (23 Ansari Road),
Darya Ganj, New Delhi - 110 002 (India).
Phones : 23245001 / 02 / 03 / 04.
Fax : +91-11-23245005.
E-mail : books@academicfoundation.com
www.academicfoundation.com

in association with the
Observer Research Foundation, New Delhi

Cataloging in Publication Data--DK
Courtesy: D.K. Agencies (P) Ltd. <docinfo@dkagencies.com>

China today : politics, society & culture.
p. cm. -- (ORF China studies series ; 1)
Contributed articles.

ISBN 13: 9788171888931
ISBN 10: 8171888933

1. China--Politics and government--21st century. 2. China--Social conditions--21st century. I. Observer Research Foundation. II. Series: ORF China studies series ; 1.

DDC 320.951 23

Typeset by Italics India, New Delhi.
Printed and bound in India.

Contents

About the Editor/Contributors

Editor:

M. Rasgotra, President, ORF-Centre for International Relations, was decorated with the Padma Bhushan in 2002. Educated at Government College, Lahore, he joined Indian Foreign Services in September 1949. In the pioneering Indian diplomacy, he served with distinction in Indian missions in Washington D.C., Kathmandu and in the Ministry of External Affairs. From 1958 to 1962, he made a notable contribution in the evolution and implementation of India's policies towards her neighbours. His Ambassadorial career took him to Morocco and Tunisia, the USA, Britain, Nepal, the Netherlands, France and UNESCO. His tenure as Foreign Secretary (1982 to 1985) was marked by a renewal in Indo-American relations, sustained negotiations with Pakistan and a tentative opening to China. He played a significant role at the prestigious events of the Seventh Non-Aligned Summit, the Commonwealth Heads of Government Meeting, the Six-Nation Appeal on Nuclear Disarmament and the Six-Nation Summit at New Delhi.

After retirement, he was Honorary Visiting Professor, Jawaharlal Nehru University, New Delhi, Regents' Professor at University of California, Los Angeles (UCLA) and President, Delhi College of Arts & Commerce, New Delhi. He is founder President of the International Institute of Asia-Pacific Studies. Through his numerous articles, lectures and his commentaries on Indian and foreign electronic media, he continues to make an important contribution to national thinking of foreign policy and security related matters.

Contributors:

Ravi Bhoothalingam studied Experimental Psychology at Cambridge University, UK. After holding senior positions in industry in India and overseas, he now serves on several company boards and travels extensively in China, Mongolia and High Asia to promote cultural and business ties.

Raviprasad Narayanan is Assistant Research Fellow at the Institute of International Relations (IIR), National Chengchi University, Taiwan. He has published many articles in newspapers and magazines and contributed chapters and research papers to books and journals in India and abroad.

K. Raghunath, former Foreign Secretary of India, served as Ambassador to Russia, Nigeria and the Philippines. He specialises on India-China relations.

D.S. Rajan retired as China Analyst, Cabinet Secretariat, Government of India. He was posted to Indian missions in Hong Kong, Tokyo and Beijing during service. He is presently Director of the Chennai Centre of China Studies. He has been regularly contributing articles on China to various journals and publications.

C.V. Ranganathan has been Ambassador of India to various countries, including China and France. Since his retirement from the Indian Foreign Service in 1993, he has held various advisory and research positions. He also served as convener of the National Security Advisory Board. He has published many articles and contributed to books, newspapers, journals and magazines in India and abroad on international affairs. He has co-authored a book, *India and China—The Way Ahead* (2010).

Ravni Thakur is Professor of Chinese Studies at the Department of East Asian Studies, Delhi University. She has published widely in reputed academic journals and published under Zed Books. She is also Assistant Secretary for International Relations, Congress Party.

Foreword

This book forms part of the Observer Research Foundation's ongoing study of all aspects of developments in China, India's great neighbour, its likely future political and social evolution, its economy and how its foreign and security policies affect India and the world.

There are very thorough studies being undertaken in the United States and several countries in Europe and Asia. There is also a certain amount of good work being done on China in some Indian universities, by scholars and former diplomats who have had direct personal experience of China: but all of it put together is far from enough. To be properly understood, this huge and powerful country, the cradle of an ancient and evolving civilisation, demands a much more sustained and methodical study. We in India need to know China better.

ORF's China Studies programme is an effort in that direction. This volume is a collection of analytical papers on the current internal political, social and cultural scene of China by Indian experts whom we brought together in a seminar at ORF. The proceedings of three more seminars, on China's economy and foreign and security policies, and China's policies towards India's South Asian neighbours, will also be published as a part of this series in the course of the next 12 months.

I take this opportunity to thank the authors who have contributed to this volume.

While the Foundation has encouraged freedom of expression of all points of view in this book and in its other publications, the authors alone are responsible for the facts and opinions expressed in their contributions. That is to say, they do not necessarily reflect the views of the ORF.

—M. Rasgotra

President,

ORF Centre for International Relations

Introduction

K. Raghunath

The primary focus of our study of present-day China is:

(a) To understand how and why the totality and specific aspects of China's intentions and actions, as well as developments relating to China impinge on our national interests.

(b) To factor this assessment into working out a sensible relationship with China.

This exercise requires identifying accurately the mainsprings of Chinese thinking and conduct, and the circumstances shaping them. China's regional and global interactions are of course, an essential part of this conditioning milieu. An even more fundamental and decisive element is China's internal dynamic—i.e., China's politics, society, culture, economy and national ethos. The foreign policy and foreign relations of any country are strongly influenced by domestic imperatives (even as governments strive to ensure that this influence does not work contrary to national interest). China's internal dynamic crucially determines external behaviour, and to understand the latter, one has to see China 'inside out'—as one observer puts it. This truism bears reiteration because it is not always adequately recognised—despite the importance we attach to understanding China.

In key attributes, such as territorial expanse, demography, traditional socioeconomic make up, civilisational character and status, as well as modern developmental tasks and global challenges, China is comparable to India, perhaps more than any other country.

Learning from, and sharing our experience with China is rightly upheld as a very worthwhile venture. In this context too, it is essential that we correctly read China's politics, society, culture and economy. Moreover, this has to be done not merely in the immediate focus of current events, but also in the larger perspective of China's history, language and culture. A clear grasp of this principle is a major factor contributing to the quality of contemporary China studies in the West and other countries, e.g., in East and Southeast Asia.

A major objective of China studies is to assess China's overall prospects—short, medium and long-term. Such prognoses require taking stock of China's performance record, and in particular, its national strengths and vulnerabilities. This exercise also demands an accurate and thorough grasp of China's internal dynamic. China's historical self-image of a Middle Kingdom reigning supreme, proved hollow when confronted by Western military and economic power, because the genuine national strength on which this had been built over the centuries, had declined greatly by the time of the Western colonial era, even though the Middle Kingdom myth was kept alive by China's rulers and ideologues. Is it being revived now in a new form, with the purpose of once again projecting a model of superior national power and unassailable strategic superiority—in the first instance, in relation to the large Asian neighbourhood? And if so, is China's 'comprehensive national strength', to use their own terminology, also being built purposefully to sustain this aspiration? How is this related to China's new nationalism—frequently commented on, and also seen by many as resurgent? These fundamental questions call for a proper comprehension of what happens inside China to be seen objectively and without putting an exaggerated strategic connotation on every event and decision. We should also retain a sense of China as a leading civilisation and modern nation.

It is in keeping with these guidelines, that in the seminar series mentioned in the foreword, the internal situation in China is being taken up as the first aspect to be studied, prior to, and in preparation for assessments of other themes, such as foreign policy, and India-China relations. This is the framework in which this compilation of papers dealing with different aspects of China's politics, society and culture has been put together. For convenience of treatment, the Chinese economy, which is obviously an integrally linked aspect of the internal situation, is addressed in a separate set of papers. The authors of the articles in this volume, though not dealing directly with the economic dimension, have kept it in constant view.

The study of China's internal situation, taken up in this compilation, must above all, give us an idea of the real time ground situation inside China. This is not an abstract exercise; the analysis should provide a sense of quality and direction of Chinese politics, society and culture—e.g., how state power functions and to what ends; the state of the people's welfare, prosperity and morale; political and social change and other large themes. For this purpose, several key questions need to be addressed, and answers found—however tentative, such as the following: (These questions are listed here as indicative, not exhaustive lines of enquiry: the observations made below are suggestions for provoking thought, rather than an attempt at comprehensive analysis).

i) A striking, and dominant feature of politics in present day China is, that right from the founding of the People's Republic of China (PRC), down to the present day, national leadership, political power and control have continuously been in the hands of the Communist Party of China (CCP)—periodical, inner Party dissensions notwithstanding. How has this come about? How has China remained almost the sole exception to the history of the entire Socialist world—i.e., collapse of Communist Party-based political power systems, and transition, however imperfect, to recognisably democratic structures (or in exceptional cases, dysfunctional prolongation of the old system, as in North Korea).

ii) This has been made possible, in the first place, because of the realisation within the leadership in the immediate aftermath of the Mao era, that without ensuring meaningful economic growth, including, in particular, measurable prosperity for the citizen, a less constricted system of governance, as well as some opening up to the outside world, not only would China remain backward and weak, but the credibility of the CCP leadership would itself be seriously eroded.

iii) There is no doubt that the gathering protest mood of the 1980s, culminating in the Tiananmen confrontation, followed soon thereafter by the collapse of the Soviet Union, and the worldwide trend towards democracy, shook the Chinese leadership, and brought home to them that if they failed to carry out basic changes, not only their credibility, but their political survival would be at risk.

The fundamental new guidelines worked out by them—from the 1980s on through the 1990s were, essentially—active promotion of the private sector, and specifically, entrepreneurship; far reaching economic reform and liberalisation; strong encouragement of wealth creation ('it is glorious to be rich'); embracing economic globalisation in a big way; recognising that it was crucial to stimulate efficient economic growth in China; progressive (and regulated) geographical decentralisation of economic management and investment; strong support to innovation and R&D; development of a pragmatic, multidirectional foreign policy, in contrast to Mao era isolation and constriction, and dramatic changes in alignment from one super power to the other.

(iv) All this represents a departure from Mao era doctrines and policies, which are much more radical and substantive than the hesitant, and often opportunistic deviation from ideological orthodoxy made by other Socialistic regimes—especially in their declining years. At the same time, while jettisoning a good deal of orthodox Marxist Leninist and Maoist ideology, the CCP has retained, almost in entirety, the orthodox Socialist/Maoist power structure, organisation, instruments and mechanisms of control and regulation by the Party, and even procedure and nomenclature. This could be explained, in the first instance by the reformers' awareness, that theirs was a venture into the unknown with imponderable risks, and would therefore have to be a calibrated effort under effective Party control and discipline. What better milieu could there be to ensure this, than continuance of the tried and tested Communist Party regime? Even more important, the desired perpetuation of the hold on power by the ruling Communist Party elite, renewed from one political generation to the next, could be ensured only by continuing Party control in reinforced and streamlined form.

This brings us closer to an understanding of what the post Mao political and power dispensation is all about. How is one to characterise a political system which has discarded much of Communist ideology in the critical matter of economic policy and practice, but retained the traditional Communist Party power structure almost in entirety? In answer, consider the following:

(i) Perhaps to a much greater extent than in other systems, Communist Party power structures in the erstwhile Socialist world have had to work under a compulsion to ensure continuation in power of the elite ruling group and dominance of the Party for the purpose of ensuring effective implementation of their national development programmes and reasserting national pride and influence and not least, for personal power aggrandisement. Perhaps more than in democratic power systems, in the Socialist world, ideology has very much been a convenient means to this end, to be flexibly defined and analysed as required by the power agenda. The distinctive point about China is that while in almost all the other Socialist states the ruling Party failed to sustain this act, leading to eventual collapse of their systems, the CCP has succeeded in junking much of doctrinal orthodoxy in substance (above all economic) while also claiming to be a defender of orthodoxy, retaining very substantial elements of the Communist Party centred-political system. One of many striking illustrations of this is that while actively promoting entrepreneurship, the CCP has also nurtured a huge state capitalist sector deploying huge assets, i.e., not merely the traditional old fashioned public sector units (PSUs), but refurbished mega-state companies—working in a globalised era, especially in energy and other infrastructure.

(ii) This development was expectedly marked by hectic inner Party debates i.e., in the 1980s between Left and Right, the diehard Maoist old guard *versus* the reformers, as well as personality-based power struggles, (recall the dramatic leadership changes of the 1980s). Subsequently, in the 1990s and thereafter, the inner Party struggle came to be waged between technocrat-politicians with differing agendas for development, again reflecting, as always, personality-based power struggles.

The CCP leadership appears to date, to have succeeded in working out via media which has preserved the formula consisting on the one hand, of liberalised economic policy and delivery of good governance, and on the other, reinforced Party control and regulation, and a restrictive but not necessarily an oppressive regime which permitted limited freedom (e.g. media)—with many co-optive elements. They also continue to promote the image of being custodians of doctrinal orthodoxy even while promoting radical reforms ('Socialism with Chinese characteristics').

This dispensation can plausibly be credited with facilitating and spearheading China's considerable national achievements over this period: in the first place, sustained, high, and even spectacular economic growth; booming, entrepreneurial activity, steady progress in S&T and innovation, characterised by successful linking with industry and agriculture; huge infrastructural development; building of a large export market, and consequent large surpluses and sovereign funds, which have given China great economic and political clout; steadily widening prosperity, including the lifting of millions from below the poverty line; political stability and effective governance, especially law and order; large scale military capabilities; extended global reach and enhanced prestige; recognition of China as a pre-eminent, resurgent power, and driver of Asia Pacific economic growth; and a country beginning to help set the tone for reforming an international system put in place under Western inspiration, now displaying many flaws. Because of the benefits China's growth has brought, as summed up above, there has been considerable popular acceptance of, and participation, in the new national order.

The key question is whether this overall political-economic model and power structure has any basic weaknesses which could slow down, or undermine China's seemingly unstoppable growth—or perhaps even cause a collapse of the Chinese system.

This core issue has to be addressed in the context of the acute political, economic and social stresses and strains, which reforms, liberalisation and globalisation have inescapably brought. While India itself is a prime example, in China's case, these are from all indications compounded by even greater popular expectations generated by China's highly acclaimed growth, and the self-imposed striving for regional and global power status. The tensions and contradictions expected in a period of rapid growth anywhere appear to be that more accentuated in China than elsewhere. China has depended considerably on a performance-oriented elite for spearheading economic/technological growth. This has generated an even more acute increase in socioeconomic inequalities, differentials between rich and poor, town and country, the professionally educated elite and the rest, the privileged and the marginalised. Globalisation unstoppable and impersonal, has exacerbated social tensions and contradictions. The indication that those at the lower rungs of the ladder in China are better off than their counterparts in India or in other comparable countries, does not minimise China's problem on this front.

This dynamic is well reflected in the recurrent widespread and apparently serious protests in different sections of Chinese society—which are being reported prominently in the West, and also feature regularly in the Chinese media. Much of this unrest is generated by victims of injustice—i.e., of bureaucracy, local political bosses, corruption including the large scale variety caused by mafia, said to be active especially in high profile megapolises such as Chongqing; the huge army of urban migrant workers; others who are marginalised and the dispossessed—e.g., victims of land acquisition, of environmental damage (usually collateral). Besides these, one has to think of religious sects (e.g. Falun Gong) and ethnic minorities (notably Tibet and Sinkiang). Further, a large number of special constituencies which have collectively enabled the Chinese economic miracle—i.e., professionals, technocrats, managers, S&T workers, leaders in the arts & culture, environmentalists and, even people within the power structure have also emerged as articulate and credible critics of the establishment. Yet another category of the disapproving is that of the ultra nationalists who applaud China's rise, but feel that the leadership is still not assertive enough on the external front e.g., *vis-à-vis* the US, Japan and the West generally. Add to this the less friendly opponents of the regimes—i.e., dissidents among the intelligentsia, youth and parts of the mass media, i.e., constituencies which have made a major issue of the CCP's 'democracy deficit'. One needs to examine the playing out and net impact of these diverse trends.

The leadership is no doubt aware of the threat which these various kinds of discontent and unrest, including that prompted by rising popular expectations fed by the very success of the regime, poses for economic growth, political/social stability and to their own position. In this context, we must consider the conventional wisdom that the CCP regime derives its legitimacy largely from the popular recognition of the economic growth, prosperity, good governance, stability, security and global prestige that it has brought to China. It is implied that any serious setbacks on these fronts could undermine the leadership's popular acceptance and standing and call its mandate into questions. It would be a fair to surmise that the CCP leadership would not want any of this to be a self-fulfilling prophecy and therefore puts the highest priority to safeguarding the system.

There is ample indication that in this framework, the Hu-Wen leadership attaches the high priority to rectify the imbalance in favour of gross economic growth, as against genuine development, quality of life, social justice and equity. The totalitarian Maoist Communist regime might be discredited, but issues of social stability/justice they grappled with are still with China, and it is noteworthy that as elsewhere in the world, some of the remedies of the earlier era are now being invoked. The Hu-Wen leadership is distinctively identified with a range of policy measures for guaranteeing social justice and public welfare—and by helping the less privileged constituencies listed above. There is also a special effort to show solicitude for the large numbers hit by China's periodic national disasters. The government has also taken many populist measures. In particular, there is an increased show of willingness to take public grievances on board, not excluding the demand for more democracy. Thus, the leadership has on its own initiative, engaged with the public in an open debate on this theme, suggesting a calibrated move towards greater democratisation, starting from the grassroots, e.g. with basic level local elections. Not surprisingly, these conciliatory moves are subsumed in a larger framework of building a 'harmonious' society, obviously meant to underline the need for a balance between freedom and discipline—between authority and democracy.

In evaluating the sustainability of this model and the agenda of 'benevolent authoritarianism', one must in the first place, identify, the generic and universal features of the system, and its problem and challenges as against what is exceptional and unique to China. The former includes almost the entire menu of people's protests—which are largely familiar and common to all countries of comparable size, above all India, which are engaged in bringing about rapid economic growth and modernisation. Expectedly, many of the responses of the Chinese leadership are also generic and universal. The exceptional and unique feature of the Chinese situation is, that unlike India and others working in a recognisably democratic political framework to bring about rapid economic growth, China continues to do this with a largely Communist Party political structure. The conventional wisdom is that a democratic framework enables discontent and unrest to be absorbed and internalised, and has built-in space for peaceful resolution of problems. The 'million mutinies of India', are arguably in the last analysis not an indication of a state of all round revolt, but rather an exercise in freedom of expression, a phenomenon which can be dealt with constructively without the system being unduly stressed. Protest in a democracy is a safety valve and wake up call which the system is expected to take to heart, whereas in a cast-iron authoritarian set up, there is much less flexibility and a narrower margin for dealing with them. How accurate is this perception and is it a reasonably good guide to understanding China's unrest?

Some would argue that the differences between the Chinese and the more democratic variants, in regard to popular discontent, notably India, should not be exaggerated. The acid test is whether disequilibrium in a system connotes instability, or can it be taken in one's stride. Protests in China have been described by some observers as a case of 'dynamic stability', much the same as elsewhere and fulfilling the same purpose. The Chinese leadership, it could be argued has adopted a sound approach, in that stresses good governance and law and order, public safety and welfare, and all-round economic prosperity as a prior requirement, without which democracy remains a meaningless, propagandistic slogan which could even be counterproductive.

According to this view, the Chinese leadership is indeed responsive to popular opinion—if for no other reason, than the fact that as an authoritarian regime, it is concerned about its legitimacy and mandate being vitiated by setbacks to economic growth and governance. They are in fact groping their way to finding an optimal political system, 'crossing the river by feeling the stones' to quote a familiar Chinese proverb, and are gradually broadening basic freedoms, moving towards more constitutional accountability to the people and a normal, more open rather than an over-calibrated, managed democracy—which is the current goal. With this evolutionary dynamic at work, the CCP itself through the ultimate logic of its own programmes, might well morph into a different and more open structure, eventually with a suitable change in nomenclature and organisation, reflecting its relinquishment of the monopoly of power in due course. The implication of this perception of China, is that it has already put in place changes in the political/social system which are working to make it more democratic and responsive, and one needs to correct an obsessive concern with the Communist Party's monopolistic control.

On the contrary, a hard-headed view is that the dominant dynamic and force driving politics in present day China is the CCP leadership's powerful compulsion to stay in power (with generational change in personalities, no doubt, but within the same structure). The best construction on their motivation is that they wish above all to remain and entrusted and empowered with the task of taking China forward, on the basis of their agenda for economic growth, governance and comprehensive national development and building China into a superpower. Bold experiments in economic policy/management are imperative—but they would not want to risk entering new political turf, least of all democratisation, especially when there is no compelling need for this. It appears true that Chinese policies have evolved from the harsh 'Legalist' authoritarianism of the Mao era to a more benevolent 'Confucian' ethos—but even the latter is paternalistic, not entirely trustful of the people's ability to decide for themselves. Hence the present leadership system has strong in-built resistance to diluting their power monopoly.

The consequence of this attachment to power in a non-democratic system is continued distortion in decision-making, and perpetuation of dysfunctional institutions and mechanisms that must be reformed to ensure economic efficiency—a notable example would be the state capitalist empire. An equally serious concern is that the Party, far from diminishing, is growing in membership and reach, with an emphasis on co-option, and continues to be a mammoth organisation. It has grown into a stupendously rich and complex institution and is pre-eminently a power entity. This is not the kind of Party that is likely to dissolve itself or abdicate its authority or morph in something gentler. The logical conclusion from these premises is that the Party's power monopoly could be of diminishing utility as a driver of China's national development and even of crude economic growth; it could in fact hamper realisation of China's full potential and the Party's own evolution could well be a traumatic rather than a normal, gradual process.

One can add to this prognosis the possibility that China's relentless growth of national power, could intensify ultra nationalist sentiment, as well as militarism—as a force shaping policy—e.g. demands that the leadership should be more assertive in international affairs, *vis-à-vis* countries such as the US, Japan and probably India. The leadership's responses could well turn to a populist cultivation of nationalism, rather than a check on extremism. These outcomes could well pervert Chinese national direction in a manner comparable to that of ascendant powers in earlier eras, e.g. in Europe.

These are alternative scenarios to be examined objectively—with an informed and not a speculative approach. In this exercise, one has to consider the premise that China has a very long tradition of civilisational good sense and of internal political social mechanisms that help preserve a balance—i.e., the golden mean.

An important complex of specific questions—to be addressed in the broad framework just outlined above—is the special challenge of governing a country with such large territory, marked by great diversity, geographical as well as ethnic. Till well into the 20th century, China was afflicted by chronic warlordism and there were powerful regional 'bosses' even in Han majority provinces, defying central authority. In today's context, this translates into the Centre's compulsion to tolerate strong regional Party leaders, whose power is based on the great resources and the large expanse of their respective domains. China also continues to contend with growth differentials between the advanced coastal provinces and the relatively backward interior especially the Northwest and West and between the mega cities and villages. Another related dimension in the distinctive geographical and demographic make up of China—i.e., over 40 per cent of its area is composed of very large highly resource rich, but remote and sparsely populated, and relatively poor regions—notably Tibet and Sinkiang. Dealing with the unique problem of integrating these strategically crucial provinces is still a 'work in progress'. Will the central leadership succeed in fully integrating and pacifying these provinces through its ongoing programme which emphasises energetic building of connectivity and rapid economic development, along with special incentives and concessions to regional sentiment and pride?

Among other core issues and themes are: i) role of the PLA in political/strategic decision-making and civil-military relations, ii) the functioning of the judicial and legal systems in China moving at a satisfactory pace, towards government by laws and not by men, (iii) clarity on the state of civil society, of the mass media, the role of internet, iv) large trends in the arts and culture, and their interactions with the political systems and v) the state of religion and religious freedom.

Part of the standard drill of China-watching is the regular monitoring and analysis of Party Congresses, NPC and other meetings—which formalise and confirm leadership concerns and decisions, as well as trends in policy and personnel. This is of obvious relevance to understanding the internal system in China.

The first paper is an overview of the broad themes and issues flagged above. The second focusses in greater detail on the questions regarding the leadership and the political system noted above. The third is a detailed field study-based narrative, and assessment of socioeconomic trends, tensions and contradictions and popular/government responses. The fourth treats the same issue—on a broader canvas—of the impact of globalisation on Chinese politics and society, and how China is dealing with this challenge. The fifth and last paper is on unorthodox addition to this compilation—i.e., an examination of cultural and civilisational traits, as reflected in the Chinese language and their bearing on politics and society and on foreign policy.

1 Internal Political Scene in China

An Overview

D.S. Rajan

The People's Republic of China (PRC) is in the hands of a collective leadership, which makes policies through consensus; this situation is in contrast to that witnessed in the past—single supreme leaders (Mao Zedong, Deng Xiaoping and Jiang Zemin) dominated politics as the 'core' of the respective regimes. The trend towards a rule by a collective was confirmed in the 17th Congress of the Chinese Communist Party (CCP) (Beijing, October 15-21, 2007); no serious setback to it has been seen till today. Secondly, it is becoming clear, especially since the Congress, that the 'fourth generation' CCP General Secretary Hu Jintao-Premier Wen Jiabao leadership is consolidating its position and that there is no major impediment to implementation of their policies aimed at moving away from an investment and export driven economy to expansion of domestic consumption. Hu's 'scientific outlook on development', on which the policies rest in ideological terms, now figures in the CCP Constitution. Favourable conditions seem to be gradually emerging for leadership succession by the 'fifth generation' leaders in 2012, when the next Party Congress is due. However, the failure to appoint Vice President Xi Jinping, believed to be a strong candidate to succeed Hu Jintao as Party chief, as First Central Military Commission (CMC) Vice-Chairman during the latest Party conclave, may signal a lack of leadership consensus at present on the military role that can be given to the former. This raises the question whether the transfer of power in 2012 will really be problem-free.

Future Leadership

In keeping with the norm of retirement at 68, both Hu and Wen, among others, are expected to leave their offices in 2012. What will be the leadership line-up in that year and thereafter? The 17th Party Congress gave valuable clues in this regard by making four new appointments to the nine-member top policymaking body—the Politburo Standing Committee (PBSC). Out of them, two—Xi Jinping who ranks sixth in the PBSC, but listed first among the four newcomers, and Li Keqiang are widely expected to succeed the Hu-Wen leadership. They were elevated directly to the PBSC without serving as members of the Politburo (Miller, 2008). The National People's Congress (NPC) in 2008, had elected Xi as Vice-President and Li as Executive Vice-Premier. The assumption of office by Xi Jinping and Li Keqiang respectively as Party General Secretary (in 2012) and Prime Minister (2013), is a distinct possibility. Two other new PBSC members, He Guoqiang and Zhou Yonggang, are cadres with a background in the petroleum industry; this would be significant, considering that China's challenges in future includes energy security.

Just who are Xi Jinping and Li Keqiang, the apparent heirs to the Hu-Wen regime? Xi is the son of former revolutionary leader Xi Zhongxun and thus represents what has been named as the 'Princeling' group in the Party. He holds a doctorate degree in law from the prestigious Tsinghua University and is believed to support large and rapid growth in GDP. Li Keqiang's career includes considerable experience in services in the more backward regions. This appears to have strengthened his belief on the importance of balanced economic development.

The Mao era was led by a revolutionary generation and under Deng Xiaoping and Jiang Zemin, the leadership was largely technocratic. The new PBSC is by all indications less technocratic, with half its members more broadly trained in economy and legal fields.

Further, the new leadership which emerged from the 17th Congress seems to be free from the old factional differences (like Shanghai clique *versus* the rest). If at all there is a division, it could be between those having had strong links with the past leadership and those enjoying grassroot support[1] (one could place five in the first category—Wu Bangguo, Jia Qinglin, Li Changchun, Xi Jinping and Zhou Yonggang and four in the latter—Hu Jintao,Wen Jiabao, He Guoqiang and Li Keqiang). The new

1. Kerry Brown, Royal Institute of International Affairs online, 2007.

PBSC appears to be made up of 'elitists' with a bias in favour of the market and entrepreneurship (Wu Bangguo, Jia Qinglin and Xi Jinping) and 'populists' who pay attention to poor and backward regions (Hu Jintao, Wen Jiabao, Li Keqiang).[2] Overall, there appears to be a general consensus among the nine top Chinese leaders on the core agenda—reforms, social equality, environment and the supremacy of the CCP.

During his second term as Party chief, Hu Jintao has been successful in consolidating power through appointing his loyalists both at the Centre and provinces, who invariably have grassroots level experience and ties with Communist Youth League (CYL), which was once led by him. The case of Central Committee departments is an example—persons owing allegiance to Hu are now in charge (Ling Jihua in the Party General Office, Li Yuanchao in the Organisation Department, Liu Yunshan in the Propaganda Department, Du Qinglin in United Front Work Department, Wang Jiarui in the International Department and Wang Huning in Policy Research Office).[3] Since the last Party Congress, personnel close to Hu Jintao have taken over top Party and government posts in many provinces, including Shanghai, Hebei, Heilungjiang, Guangdong and Chongqing municipality. Better-educated officials with modern business management experience and skills seem to be getting preference.[4]

Democracy

There are signs of the Hu-Wen regime having chosen to introduce some form of inner Party democracy. In the last Party Congress, Hu asked for the introduction of a tenure system for delegates to the Party congresses at all levels, open selection and competition for Party positions, multi-candidate elections and prevention of 'arbitrary decision-making by an individual or minority of people'. Hu, at the same time, has admitted deficiencies in 'democratic legal building'. Grassroots Party elections in villages introduced a decade ago, though marked initial steps towards direct democracy, turned out to be a failure, as village officials remained unwilling to lose their control through elections.

2. Li (2009).

3. China Leadership Monitor (2009), No.27, Winter.

4. *www.china.org.cn*, 14 January 2008.

As far as Chinese society is concerned, the Hu-Wen leadership model is based on 'Socialist Political Democracy with Chinese Characteristics' led by the CCP. The first official White Paper on Democracy (19 October 2005) focussed on the same theme. Since then, the CCP has repeatedly disapproved of the Western type of democracy being suitable for China, the latest instance being PBSC member Wu Bangguo's remarks at the National People's Congress in March 2009.

It is interesting that notwithstanding the CCP's categorical position on democracy, a debate among intellectuals on the subject is in progress, *albeit* with the tacit approval of the authorities. (For example articles on 'Democracy is a Good Thing for China',[5] 'Democracy will prevail',[6] 'Seeking truth cannot be separated from "freedom of speech"',[7] and a rejoinder entitled 'Only Democratic Socialism can Save China'[8] have been published). China's intellectuals appear divided into three camps—(i) a 'Neo-left' group that wants a state-regulated market economy and opposes privatisation, marketisation and globalisation[9] (like Prof. Wang Hui, Qinghua University), (ii) a 'Neo-liberal' one favouring a gradual liberalisation process for China (like Prof. Zhou Ruijin, former editor of the *People's Daily,* Du Daozheng, editor of *Yanhuang Chunqiu* journal which sympathises with the ideas of former ousted Party chief Zhao Ziyang, Prof. Shen Minde of the Communication University of China and Li Rui, Mao's one time Secretary), and (iii) an ultra-leftist group with allegiance to 'Mao Zedong thought' represented by websites like *Maoflag*.

Giving expression to 'neo-liberal' ideas, last year a group of intellectuals presented a 'Declaration of Human Rights' Charter to the authorities, which came to the outside world as 'Charter 2008'. This demands among other things a new constitution for China providing for competitive elections. The CCP's tolerance of different ideological streams

---

5. Yu Keli, *Foreign Affairs*, May/June 2009. Yu in the article rejects western democratic models for China.
6. Zhang Wen, China Elections and Governance website, 9 January 2009. Zhang sees confrontation between democracy and socialism with Chinese characteristics, with the possibility of latter getting defeated one day.
7. Shen Minde, *Beijing Daily*, 13 January 2009.
8. Tao (2007).
9. He (2008) and Hook (2007).

has been manifested as its 'letting hundred flowers bloom and hundred schools of thought contend, as long as the country's unity and stability is not jeopardised.'[10] On the whole, the CCP seems to perceive that at a time when China is undergoing a massive transformation, such open discussions may lead to generation of ideas useful as policy inputs. The indication is that Hu Jintao's concept of a 'harmonious society' for China echoes 'Neo-left' concerns, and the Eleventh Five-Year Plan (2006-2010) could be seen as signifying Beijing's efforts to accommodate both 'Neo-left' and 'Neo-liberal' ideas.

Military

Fundamental changes in civil-military relations are taking place in the PRC. The 'Party commands the gun' remains the key principle of the ruling CCP in dealing with the People's Liberation Army (PLA); on the other hand, civilian supremacy over politics is also growing day by day in China and the political influence once enjoyed by the PLA, is diminishing. The present low representation of the PLA in the top Party organs, except in Central Military Commission (CMC), makes the military's declining political role evident. There is no PLA representative in the PBSC; in the 25-member Politburo, 22 have no military background, and the powerful Party Secretariat has no PLA representation. This gives us the impression that a process is on to keep the Army apolitical and restricts it to a narrow professional focus, i.e., on military affairs. The composition of the core is in itself instructive; except Hu Jintao, it has no other PBSC member; in particular, in a departure from past practice, there is no First Vice-Chairman in the core and even Xi Jinping, considered as heir-apparent to Hu as Party chief (in 2012) is not yet a member of the CMC. Contrary to expectations, the just held Fourth Plenum of the 17th CCP Central Committee (Beijing, 15 to 18 September 2009) did not appoint him to the post of the First CMC Vice-Chairman. This gap in the top military structure may create problems for control over the CMC in future by the upcoming next generation of Party leadership. Certain key factors underlying the diminishing role of the PLA would include the absence of a paramount leader, generational shifts in the civilian and military

10. Qiu Shi, 16 July 2009.

leaderships, increasing professionalism in the military and sustained progress in economic development (Tam, 2006).

As an important trend, young and technocratic officers are rising rapidly in the PLA; this has implications for military modernisation efforts (Cheng and Harold, 2008). This is happening along with a high rate of turnover in their positions, for e.g. 60 per cent of the military forces in the 17th Central Committee are new; this turnover could signal efforts to prevent the rise of strong military figures.

In the circumstances outlined above, the demands being made by some for a 'nationalised army' in the country are not unexpected. The CCP itself has acknowledged the existence of such differences in opinions, along with a heavy stress on the need for following the principle of 'party's absolute leadership over army'. Hu Jintao and top military leaders continue to emphasise this principle. Notable is the call given at a CMC meeting presided by Hu (Xinhua, 1 February 2009) to all military forces to 'unify their will to the decision and deployment of the CPC Central Committee to ensure that they uncompromisingly follow the Party and Central Military Commission's command at any time and under any circumstances'. A recent article by General Li Jinai, a CMC member in the Party's theoretical organ *Qiu Shi* (1 April 2009) exhorted the military to 'resolutely oppose the wrong thinking represented by concepts such as army-Party separation, depoliticisation, and army nationalisation'.

It should however be noted that the theme of 'CCP's absolute leadership over the army', is not new in China. It had figured in the pre-revolutionary days (the Mao Zedong-Zhang Guodtao rift on Party-military ties in the late 1930s which led to the latter's expulsion from the CCP allegedly on charges of favouring Party-army separation). In the post-liberation period, during the 'anti-rightist' campaign of the late 1950s, there were allegations of 'monolithic military thoughts' prevailing in the Party with some even preferring 'liquidation of Party committees in the military'.[11] In the 1980s and the early 1990s, there were reports on support to a 'nationalised' army, coming from advisers to Premier Zhao Ziyang as well as some other sections of the leadership (Swaine, 2005). Subsequently,

11. Liberation Army Daily, 1 July 1959 and 17 August 1959.

one saw possible indications, challenges to the Party in enforcing control over the army, lack of enthusiasm on the part of some PLA men in dealing with the 1989 Tiananmen student protests,[12] the closure of PLA-led enterprises in 1998 following Premier Zhu Rongji's dissatisfaction over the army's alleged smuggling activities, the observation of Qiao Shi, NPC Standing Committee Chairman (Le Figaro, April 1997) that President and CMC chief Jiang Zemin should be answerable to Parliament.

The emphasis on Party control over the military is evident since 2000 and, can be related to some newly emerged circumstances—cases of indiscipline in the army, such as protests by demobilised soldiers, and occasional 'independent' actions by the PLA , taken without consulting the Party and civil administration[13] (as was seen during the Sino-US EP-3 crisis of 2001 and the anti-satellite weapon test in 2007). More important, perceived apprehensions on challenges to Hu Jintao as CMC Chairman appears to originate from within the CCP. A representation indicative of this is the article by Prof. Shi Zhongquan, in the Liberation Army Daily, (19 July 2007), which asked that cadres should always remember the historical problem created by Zhang Guotao. This could well be a hint at the existence of modern day Zhang Guotaos. In an overall sense, however, any rushing to the conclusion that unity of purpose between the Party/state and the army, or for that matter within the leadership itself has been eroded would be a wrong assessment. The CMCs of the Party and state, with identical membership are designed to tackle any issue affecting such unity. Similar arrangements extend beyond the military to other fields where the Party and government are required to work in unison. For example, organisationally, under the Party Politburo, there are mechanisms like Commissions and Leading Groups (*lingdao xiaozu*) mandated to coordinate the work of several agencies and ensure Party supervision over governmental activities (e.g., central political and legal affairs commission, leading group on foreign affairs, leading group on finance and economy, leading group on rural work, leading group on Party building, leading group on Taiwan affairs, leading group on state security and leading group on science and technology).

---

12. China Daily News, Overseas edition, Taipei, 26 November 1989.
13. Mulvenon (2001) and Bajoria (2009).

Hu Jintao is continuing to consolidate his position in the military, by appointing and elevating officers of his preference. The recent appointments of Lieutenant General Chen Xiaogong, (son of former Chinese Ambassador to UN and Japan Chen Chu) as Deputy Chief of General Staff and Major General Xue Guojiang as Deputy Commander of the People's Armed Police, as well as promotion as full generals of Ma Xiaotian (son of Ma Zaiyao, formerly of PLA Political Academy), Liu Yuan (son of former President Liu Shaochi) and Zhang Haiying (son of Zhang Zhen, a former CMC Vice-Chairman and Politburo member) are prominent instances (Hsiao, 2009 and Rajan, 2009).

The main feature of China's current military build-up is its ongoing programme aimed at improving the PLA's operational capabilities—in land, sea and air. China's Defence White Paper 2008, states that the country's military modernisation will be complete by mid-21st century, and that by 2020, the PRC hopes to achieve the task of creating a more technologically advanced military that will allow it to conduct and sustain operations at a greater distance from its border. China's projection recently of its military prowess beyond the Pacific Ocean by sending small anti-piracy ships to the Gulf of Aden is an indicator in this regard. There is continuing lack of transparency in China's military funding, (the stated defence expenditure for 2007 and 2008 was US $52 billion and US $61 billion, marking on 18 per cent increase; Western sources estimate that the figure for 2008 is between US $97 to $139 billion).[14]

The prevailing image of the military in the eyes of the Chinese public also requires attention. One notes a certain uneasiness in civil society caused by deployment from time to time of the military for the purpose of tackling civilian unrest—e.g., during the 1989 student demonstrations, and the ethnic troubles in Tibet (2008) and Xinjiang (2009), though, the Chinese authorities may not admit this. At the same time, we must note the role being played by the military in winning the hearts and minds of the people through its involvement in disaster, flood relief and anti-earthquake operations in the country.

There is a growing realisation in China that without the support of society, the military cannot fulfill its modernisation objectives. It is only

14. Bajoria (2009).

society, which can offer the PLA the high calibre talent required for this purpose and the funding for research and development, essential for acquisition of modern weapons and technological systems. It is also noteworthy that there are concerns in the PLA about 'greying of society', an outcome of the government's public policy in favour of a 'one child' family; the burden in respect of benefits to military retirees has grown as a result. On its part, civil society, particularly in rural areas, is facing problems in meeting the recruitment quota fixed for them for entry into the PLA, as well as in resettling demobilised soldiers. A study (23 May 2005)[15] showed that ex-PLA men led some peasant uprisings in Hunan province.

It is not surprising that the Hu-Wen leadership is laying the theoretical foundations for the army-people unity at this juncture. Hu Jintao has revived Mao's concept of 'army-people synthesis' (Junmin Jiehe)[16] and Wen Jiabao has called for the implementation of the principle providing for 'unity between the army and government' and 'unity between army and people' (Shuangyong).[17]

Sovereignty Issues: Tibet, Xinjiang and Taiwan

China adopts an uncompromising position on all issues concerning national sovereignty. In this regard, the prevailing political situations in Tibet and Xinjiang as well as potential ethnic issues in Inner Mongolia (concerning 'three evils': terrorism, separatism and extremism) and Taiwan (centring around reunification imperative), assume special importance.

Tibet

No doubt, the large scale unrest in Tibet in March 2008 has raised questions on China's ability to exercise sovereignty over Tibet; though the scale of protests has since come down considerably, thanks to the clamping down of stern security measures by the authorities. Protests do not seem to have disappeared in the first quarter of 2009, as Khampa areas in Sichuan and some locations in Qinghai, the birth province of the Dalai Lama, have witnessed some form of civil disobedience. Meanwhile, the campaign to re-

15. Gunness (2006).
16. Xinhua, 24 July 2009.
17. Xinhua, 4 January 2008.

educate Tibetans, launched in May 2008 by the Tibet Party Secretary Zhang Qingli himself, has continued.[18]

There is also no let up in Beijing's harsh propaganda campaign against the Dalai Lama. Prominent instances have included issue of a White Paper on '50 years of Tibet Reforms' (2 March 2009) and a firm address by President Hu Jintao for building a 'Great Wall' of stability in Tibet (9 March 2009). The Dalai Lama's recent identification of the root causes for the Tibetan unrest (Geneva, 6-8 August 2009), i.e., China's autocratic rule and cultural genocide in Tibet—and observations that China's minority policy has failed to build trust among the country's nationalities has added fuel to Beijing's anti-Dalai Lama drive. Authoritative scholars and Buddhist religious leaders are in the forefront of this movement, a signed comment by Zhang Yun, China Tibetology Research Centre, Beijing, of 18 August 2009, apparently reflecting the views of the central leadership, which refers to the Dalai Lama's Geneva statement, and accuses the spiritual leader of damaging the relations between the Han and Tibetan people. A 'living Buddha' in Tibet has argued that contrary to what is being stated on behalf of the Dalai Lama, the 'incarnation of the Dalai Lama should be decided according to fixed procedures',[19] meaning thereby that incarnation should take place within China.

Interestingly, within China itself, some criticism of the Central government's policy towards Tibet has surfaced, which could well have caused embarrassment to the authorities. A Chinese group called Gongmeng (Open Constitution Initiative) has challenged (12 May 2009) the official position that the Dalai Lama incited the Tibet violence, besides alleging that China's strategies to ensure 'stability' in Tibet have failed, and that China's propaganda offensive has created divisions and further exacerbated tensions in Tibet. Such views notwithstanding, Beijing is trying to show to the outside world that every thing is normal in Tibet by inviting foreign leaders to visit Tibet (for e.g. visit to Tibet of Singapore Foreign Minister George Yeo in August 2009, the first since the March 2008 unrest

18. Unpublished speeches of Zhang Qingli, *Xigan Tongxun*, a classified party publication. *The Australian*, 14 July 2008.

19. Xinhua, Lhasa, 5 July 2009.

and a delegation of European Economic and Social Committee to Beijing and Tibet from 9 to 17 September 2009).

The visit to Dharamshala (13-14 September 2009) by a US Congressional delegation led by Valerie Jarret, Senior Adviser to President Obama, is also notable for what was reportedly conveyed to the Dalai Lama i.e., Obama's expression of support to the Dalai Lama's proposal for genuine autonomy for Tibet, for the protection of Tibetan heritage and human rights and civil liberties of Tibetans. It was indicated during the visit, that the Dalai Lama and President Obama would meet in Washington after the US-China Summit in November 2009. China has criticised the visit by declaring that it opposes any meeting between the Dalai Lama and foreign leaders (Foreign Ministry spokesperson, Beijing, 15 September 2009).

Overall, it is clear that a mismatch continues to persist between the respective stands of the two sides—the Dalai Lama's wish for genuine autonomy with Tibet being part of China, and Beijing's belief that the exiled leader has a hidden agenda for independence. The last meeting held between the Dalai Lama's envoys and the Central government at Beijing from 31 October to 5 November 2008, could not result in any agreement: the Chinese firmly rejected the Memorandum submitted by the Dalai Lama's delegation as 'another way of seeking Tibetan independence'. The Chinese assertion that the next Dalai Lama could only be born within the PRC's borders, coinciding with reported health problems of the spiritual leader, may definitely complicate further negotiations between the Dalai Lama and Beijing. It can therefore be said that there are dim prospects for a solution to the Tibet issue in the foreseeable future.

Xinjiang

The Xinjiang authorities did appear to have some premonition of the 5 July 2009 ethnic riot at Urumqi—considering the official warnings given in March 2009 itself by senior leaders that 'maintaining stability in the Northwest province this year would be a difficult task, and that militancy could spread to Xinjiang from the neighbouring countries' (Bekri, 2009).

The immediate provocation for the eruption of an Uighur-Han confrontation at Urumqi seems to be the attack on Uighur workers by

Hans in Guangdong on 25 June 2009. For three days following July 5, the situation remained tense and some normalcy was restored only after the arrival of more police and troops, especially from the Lanzhou military region which is in charge of the area. The subsequent 'syringe attacks' mostly against Hans in Urumqi, Hotan, Altay, Kashgar and other areas of Xinjiang in the first and second weeks of September 2009, affecting 531 people,[20] suggests that normalcy still eludes the Xinjiang region. According to official estimates, the number of people killed, injured and arrested during the Urumqi riots was 197, over 1,700 and 1,400 respectively. In terms of scale of civil unrests and casualty figures, the Urumqi incidents appear second only to the 1989 Tiananmen protests.

President Hu Jintao's cancellation of his G8 related engagements in Italy and return to the country on 8 July 2009 to take charge of the situation in Xinjiang, has reflected the assessment of the authorities at a national level that conditions have become urgent and serious. The leader himself toured the area (August 22-25, 2009), obviously after some gap, and his 'important' speech at Urumqi on August 25, given wide national media publicity, has been notable for its stress on ethnic unity and the need to balance reforms and stability. The CCP theoretical organ *Qiu Shi*, has commented (16 September 2009) that the speech considered the 'unity of nationalities as the lifeline of the people and important guarantee for all work relating to Xinjiang'.

Hu Jintao's abrupt return from abroad has indicated the existing weaknesses in terms of the security structure required to cope with all Urumqi-type incidents. It also has a bearing on the country's unity and stability. One notes that this may have something to do with the absence of a First Vice-Chairman of the CMC. Normally, with Hu away, the first Vice-Chairman of the CMC could have handled the situation, but this post is still vacant. Xi Jinping, said to be a successor to President Hu Jintao in 2012, could have substituted for Hu, but he is still not even a member of the CMC. Urumqi Party Secretary Li Zhi's removal from the post after the 'syringe attacks' has been the only step taken by the CCP towards fixing the responsibility at high levels. The Xinjiang Party Secretary and Politburo member Wang Lequan, in his post since 1994, so far remains untouched.

20. Xinhua, 11 September 2009.

Ethnic unrest is known to have prevailed in Xinjiang even before the Urumqi incidents. There appear to be four contributing factors—ethnic, religious, economic and political. Xinjiang (Eastern Turkestan) was independent before 1949; since the region's incorporation into the PRC in October 1949, the level of Han colonisation has been going up. The Uighurs in Xinjiang now constitutes eight million and in terms of percentage, their population which was 80 per cent in 1949 is now only 45 per cent. Regarding the religious factor, the alienation of the Uighurs has mainly been due to the prevailing restrictions on Islamic practices, ban on private visits to Mecca, and official control on mosques. Further, the Hans are enjoying business advantages, a point of dissatisfaction for Uighurs. Politically, the Hans are controlling the Party apparatus, with the post of Xinjiang Party boss always being held by a Han.

Whereas in earlier Xinjiang protests, religious extremism seemed to have played a key role, in the case of the latest Urumqi riots, the determining factor was largely racial discrimination. Also, at Urumqi, there were suicidal attacks, unlike in certain Islamic regions where such attacks are occurring with involvement of extremist groups like Al Qaeda. Admittedly, the Xinjiang authorities have described the 'syringe attacks' as 'terrorist' actions, but they do not seem to suspect any act of *Jehadi* terrorism.

Officially, the Chinese have termed the World Uighur Congress (WUC), led by Rubiya Kadeer, now in the US, as mastermind of Urumqi unrest. The state-controlled media in China have alleged that the US National Endowment for Democracy (NED) and the Holland-based Unrepresentative Peoples Organisation (UNPO) are having links with the WUC.[21] Beijing has, however, avoided any direct criticism of Washington for the Xinjiang unrest.

Inner Mongolia

There are reports of ethnic discontent in Inner Mongolia, apparently also due to Han colonisation factor. As a result of China's open door migration policy and investment drive towards Inner Mongolia, Han influx

21. People's Daily, 16 July 2009.

into the region picked up momentum and it is estimated that Hans now are 30 million as against four million Mongolians.[22] Mongolians in the province have become a minority race in their own region—only one out of five in Inner Mongolia is now an ethnic Mongolian. Two Han regions were added to Inner Mongolia in recent years in order to reduce the proportion of Mongolians to the whole regional population to 10 per cent. Dissatisfaction arose in 2001, when 650,000 Mongolian nomads and herders were forced to leave their ancestral pastures for urban areas.[23]

Beijing's Policy towards Minorities

The apparent simmering ethnic discontent in Tibet and Xinjiang and potentials for the same in Inner Mongolia, raise a basic question—how effective is the Central government's minority policy? China has 55 minority groups and their combined population is 130 million accounting for 10 per cent of the country's total population. In theory, the policy seems to be rational, providing for protection of special privileges for the minority people, along with economic benefits. The government's White Paper on minorities, issued in 2005, and its projects like the Western Area Development Programme, speak for the government's intentions. It is being argued by some analysts[24] that, 'China's present policy is based on the concept of "pragmatic nationalism", aiming at assimilation of all minority groups in the country; that is in contrast to the old theme of "ethnic nationalism", which advocated creation of a Han-led single ethnic nation'.

The main problem appears to be that the present process towards achieving population assimilation has not precluded the continuation of Han domination. Minority nationalities seem to resent this—particularly the preferential assistance to Han settlers through the government's economic projects.

22. *Tibetnet*, 5 September 2009.

23. *www.highbeam.com/doc/1G1-55693568.html*

24. Suisheng Zhao, University of Denver, 1 February 2007 and University of Southern California, US-China Institute, 14 February 2007.

Beijing's overall perspective at this juncture appears to centre round the necessity of establishing ethnic unity and stability in all minority regions, including Tibet and Xinjiang. This comes through clearly in President Hu Jintao's 'important' Urumqi speech, mentioned above, and in the call made by the Party theoretical organ *Qiu Shi* (31 August 2009) to the peoples of Tibet, Guangxi, Inner Mongolia and Ningxia to study the same speech. Simultaneously, signs of modifications in Chinese national priorities are also appearing, which need a close watch for their implications. It has been declared by China that, 'the country's first core interest is maintaining its fundamental system and state security; the second is state sovereignty and territorial integrity and the third is the continued stable development of the economy and society.'[25]

More important, Beijing's strategic concerns have come to play a predominant role in its minorities policy, particularly towards Tibet and Xinjiang. They appear to be in conformity with China's traditional perceptions that the two regions strategically located in the country's periphery, sparsely populated but occupying 40 per cent of the nation's territory and adjoining South and Central Asia, are important and such a 'periphery' needs to be secured in the overall interest of protecting the 'core' mainland inhabited by Hans. As a latest confirmation of the such perceptions, the 'Stride 2009' military exercise held in middle of August 2009, with the participation of 50,000 troops mobilised from Shenyang, Lanzhou, Jinan and Guangzhou military regions has been described as 'more important' for the situations in Tibet and Xinjiang.[26] The strategic importance of 'Southwest' region to the country found a special mention in the observations of China's Defence Minister Liang Guanglie who attended a defence mobilisation meeting organised by Chengdu Military Region (Chengdu, 29 August 2009).[27]

---

25. Statement of Dai Bingguo, China's Vice-Foreign Minister, *Zhongguo Xinwen She* (China News Agency), *www.chinanews.com.cn*, 28 July 2009, translated China Digital Times, 7 August 2009.
26. Ni Lexiong, military analyst, Shanghai, *Taipei Times*, 25 August 2009.
27. Xinhua, 29 August 2009.

Interest Groups

With the progress of economic reform, new social strata with varying interests have emerged in China; responding to these developments has become a basic internal challenge for Beijing. The most important are institutional interest groups, such as those consisting of workers of state-owned undertakings (SOEs). These are greatly affected by restructuring; indications are that they are settling their grievances through relevant administrative mechanisms. Political interest groups, like the Association for Human Rights in China, are also making their point without confronting the government. Corporate interest groups (like China Telecom) consisting of cartels are, on their part, applying pressure on the authorities to safeguard their business interests (for e.g. resisting the passing of Anti-Monopoly Law in the NPC providing for supremacy of law over industrial sectors).

Farmers losing their cultivated land and laid-off urban workers come under a different category of groups; these are involved in politically sensitive social protests to express their demands (Xin *et al.*, 2004). Though not a big threat to the government as of now, these protests are considered symbolic of opposition to social injustice. The government in the PRC is taking measures such as initiating schemes to remove rural income disparity and improve the employment climate. Annual key measures are passing of laws to abolish agriculture tax, provision of unemployment insurance and protection of private property. Of significance has been the CCP's Rural Reform and Development Plan (October 2008), which allowed Chinese farmers to lease or transfer their lands.

Judiciary

China stands for a 'socialist judicial system'. It recognises that political and judicial problems have increased, as tasks relating to national security and social stability have become more challenging.[28] In response, judicial reforms are envisaged, but no dilution in the Party's control over the judiciary can be expected as the latter is being conceived as an instrument to crackdown on dissent and maintain stability. The Party's

28. Xinhua, 18 August 2009.

Central Political and Legal Affairs Commission (CPLAC), now headed by the conservative PBSC member Zhou Yonggang, is influencing the entire judicial process. President Hu Jintao's orders in 2008 to the judiciary to follow the Party line and the warning given by CPLAC (National meeting in June 2008) that the Party's goals and concerns override everything else epitomise the Party's policy towards the judiciary.[29] According to a study, 14 provincial chief justices have had no legal training and that they run the court system in the same way as the Party and government branches function. Three principles defined for the judges while handling cases concerning social stability are—'protecting Party interests, guaranteeing interests of the people and respecting China's constitution.'[30]

Strategy to Tackle Instability

China groups the separatist movements in Tibet and Xinjiang and the activities related to Taiwan independence under one basket, indicating its view that they together pose a threat to the country's unity and security.[31] The emerging social contradictions as a result of reforms, particularly in the wake of the global financial crisis, are also being viewed in China as factors of instability. Hu Jintao has himself stated that guaranteeing the country's stability will be the 'overriding' factor (Beijing, 18 December 2008). The regime is acknowledging that the unemployment rate is rising (4.2 per cent by end of 2008 in urban areas) and that rural migrant workers out of jobs (estimated 20 million), fresh graduates and demobilised soldiers are facing sinking job prospects.[32] The CCP's legitimacy as a ruling Party will come under a test as it tackles unstable factors.

Beijing feels that the year 2009 would witness an increase in social risks and intensification of contradictions making the law and order scenario more severe and complex. Contradictions arising from the global financial crisis have interacted with the contradictions in other areas

29. Xinhua, 23 June 2008 and Lam (2008).
30. *www.china-briefing.com/news/2009/07/23/half-of-china*
31. *China Defence White Paper 2008.*
32. Ming Bao, 30 December 2008 and Xinhua, 12 January 2009.

leading to various interest groups becoming more vociferous in clamouring for their rights (Lam, 2008).

Beijing perceives that a two-pronged strategy would be necessary to protect national security and stability—strengthening professional units to counter terrorist activities and taking early steps to end social contradictions arising due to economic factors.[33] This strategy is already finding expressions at ground levels in Tibet and Xinjiang.

On the situation arising out of the global financial crisis, Beijing's recent measures appear logical—enterprises are being instructed not to lay off workers in 2009.[34] Concentration has been given to public work projects in the Government's recent US $586 billion stimulus plan; a substantial portion of the amount is earmarked for infrastructure and social sector spending in rural areas. The registered growth rate hike in the second quarter of 2009 (7.9 per cent as against the 6.1 per cent figure for the first quarter) has signalled that the stimulus programme is working well. But much would depend on the growth performance in the countryside, which remained so far neglected due to the government's preference given till recently to an export oriented industrial growth model for the country.

Conclusion

China's collective leadership, with Hu Jintao as *primus inter pares*, is by and large, functioning smoothly and the internal political situation in the country remains stable, though separatist challenges in Tibet and Xinjiang as well as the still-felt impact of the global economic crisis on the country continue to be the matters of concern to the authorities. A silver lining is the appearance of signs of a thaw in the Mainland-Taiwan relations, which may turn out to be strategically beneficial to Beijing. More important, the identification of 'fifth generation' leaders well in advance to succeed the present regime in 2012 augurs well for the PRC's political future. However, as pointed out before, some uncertainties on the scheduled power transfer in 2012 appear to have emerged following the failure to appoint Vice-President Xi Jinping, believed to be a strong

33. Xinhua, 1 February 2009.

34. Xinhua, late January 2009.

candidate to succeed Hu Jintao as Party chief, as First Central Military Commission (CMC) Vice-Chairman during the latest Party conclave indicating doubts on the military role that can be given to him. A question seems to have therefore arisen as to whether the leadership succession in 2012 will be smooth!

References

Bajoria, Jaishree (2009). "China's Military Power", *Council on Foreign Relations,* 4 February.

Bekri, Nur (2009). "Xinijiang Provincial People's Conference Chairman", *BBC Online News,* 6 March.

Cheng, Li and Scott W. Harold (2008). "China's New Military Elite", *International Herald Tribune.* January.

Gunness, Kristen A. (2006). "China's New Civil-Military Dynamic: Challenges and Opportunities for PLA Modernisation", The CNA Corporation, September.

He, Li (2008), "China's New Left and its Impact on Political Liberalization", EAI *Background Brief* No. 401, 26 August.

Hook, Leslie (2007). "Rise of China's Neo-left", *Far Eastern Economic Review* 170(3).

Hsiao, Russel (2009). "Personnel Changes in PLA Ranks: Chen Xiaogong", *China Brief* 9(3). The James Town Foundation, February 4.

Lam, Willy (2008). "The CCP's Control Over Judiciary", The James Town Foundation, 7 July.

Li, Cheng (2009). "One Party, Two Coalitions in Chinese Politics", Brookings website, 16 September.

Miller, Alice (2008). "China's New Leadership", *China Leadership Monitor,* Winter.

Mulvenon, James (2001). "Civil-Military Relations and the EP-3 Crisis—A Content Analysis", *China Leadership Monitor* 1(201), 1 September.

Rajan, D.S. (2009). "China: Speculations About a Power Struggle", *C3S Paper No*. 317, Chennai Centre for China Studies, India, 30 July.

———. (2009). "Beijing's Carrot and Stick Strategy to Tackle Instability", *China Brief* 9(3), 4 February.

Swaine, Michael D. (2005). "Civil-Military Relations: Domestic Power and Policies", *Carnegie Endowment for Peace,* 2 November.

Tam, Andrew H. (2006). "Coercion and Governance in China: Analyzing Civil—Military Relations", Monterey, CA.: Naval Post-Graduate School. March.

Tao, Xue (2007). *BBC Monitoring Service. Associated Press* 1/3/2007.

Xin, Ru, Lu Xueyi and Li Peilin (eds.) (2004). *Analysis and Forecast of China's Social Situation*. China: Chinese Academy of Social Sciences (CASS) Press. p. 235.

2 Through the Looking Glass

Trends, Developments and the Chinese Communist Party

Raviprasad Narayanan

Introduction

For the Chinese Communist Party (CCP), the calendar year 2008 was an exceptional one, oscillating between the 'manageable' and the 'unmanageable'. The 'manageable' refers to the diligence with which the CCP went about its organisational schedule of political events (the 11th National People's Congress and the Chinese People's Political Consultative Conference held in March 2008), as also the felicitous manner in which the Beijing Olympics were conducted. The 'unmanageable' refers to 'incidents'—whether due to natural or other causes—that included unusual winter storms in southern China early in the year that were followed by the catastrophic Wenchuan earthquake of May 2008. The violence that rocked Tibet in March 2008 as also the restive state of affairs in Xinjiang are challenges not only to the Party-state and its authority but also its very legitimacy. This paper explores several salient issues and seeks to interpret the CCP's agenda and actions as a methodological prism of enquiry and will focus on six lines of enquiry that identify the challenges and opportunities before the CCP as it seeks to continue its effective control over the political arena in China. These are:

i. What is the CCP and what is its relevance today?

ii. How far have the economic reforms transformed the CCP?

iii. Does the CCP profess any ideology and what are the principal themes the leadership projects to retain its hold over the 'masses'?

iv. What is the state of Central/regional-local relations in China?

v. Does the CCP consider itself as 'agent of change'?; and

vi. Is the CCP's legitimacy under threat?

What is the CCP and what is its Relevance Today?

The Party-state as an idea involves precise conceptions of both 'Party' and 'state'. A monolithic Party not only dominates the constricted political space, but also assumes for itself the role of leadership in national mobilisation and arrogates to itself an ideology that encompasses political, social and economic construction (Sartori, 1996 and Ware, 1996). In China's political culture, the 'institution' has more importance over the 'individual'. The 'state' in Chinese political culture is not an abstract concept; as an institution, its grip over all aspects of society is all-pervading. The Chinese state has traditionally made its impact felt through the effectiveness of its various organisations. The instrument of the state is used primarily to maintain social cohesion and national stability. The CCP is the primary instrument of the 'state' and vice-versa. In Hegelian terms, the CCP is the 'geist' that permeates every aspect of the state and its functions in China.

The CCP with an estimated 73 million members is the world's largest political Party. As the dominant and only visible political entity in China, with a plethora of organisational and propaganda institutions serving its needs, the CCP projects its interaction with the people at three levels—the Party as an organisation, the Party as an entity with mass of supporters, and the Party as a body of notables. With its monopoly on legitimate political organisation, the CCP reiterates its relevance by tapping into its 'residual value' based upon its indigeneous origins. In the last three decades, the CCP has made tireless efforts to display its 'accommodation' of reality by adopting a pragmatic course and jettisoning its once sacrosanct ideological shibboleths. The post Mao period has witnessed the CCP abandoning 'class struggle' in favour of economic modernisation. The era of mobilisation skills and unquestioned political reliability has given way to a new generation of Party cadres who are valued for their practical know-how, technical skills and legal aptitude (Dickson, 2006a). For many, the CCP is also a 'patronage machine'.

As the foremost 'network' controlling every aspect of state and society, the CCP remains a formidable rallying point for all kinds of actors. The attraction of membership in the CCP paves the way for appointment to public office within the state administration, career advancement within parallel or closely entwined Party-state hierarchies, as also ways of improving an individual's social and economic position (Katz and Crotty, 2006). Rather than relying on ideological mobilisation and coercion, the CCP has remained relevant by grafting new institutions—myriad types of social organisations, e.g., chambers of commerce, professional associations, sports and hobby clubs and others—that perform the role of linking state and society, as well as co-opting 'new elites' (the entrepreneurial class that has emerged in China in the reform period) into the Party. Co-option of 'new elites' permits the CCP to attract new talent with the skills and resources to enhance its functioning, and indeed its survival. Interest articulation by the CCP is channelised through a dense web of social and economic organisations that serve the purpose of regularising the flow of information between the state and key groups in society (Dickson, 2006b). This multidimensional relationship depends on the specific sector of the society one is talking about and is guided so as to support the Party's modernisation strategy (Dickson, 2003). It is estimated that around 35 per cent of private entrepreneurs are CCP members (Goodman, 2008). These include high powered corporation/enterprise heads. 'New elites' have little interest in challenging the status quo and want to integrate themselves into the political system to promote their business activities. They do not advocate broader political and social reforms, leave alone democratisation of the Party of the political system of China. At best, they would want to use their membership of the CCP to further economic reforms which would help both the Chinese economy and their own business interests.

The challenges the CCP faces are immense in scope and include issues, the resolution of which might well decide its own political future. Some of these include questions on how to liberalise the economy without destabilising the political system, how to attract new members, and how to uphold Party traditions when the reforms have brought about comprehensive change within the Party.

A significant change visible in the CCP's political culture is its stated willingness to transform itself from 'ruling Party' to 'governing Party.' The

CCP appears to be broadening its scope of learning from foreign political parties in terms of improving its capacity to govern the country. According to Wang Jiarui, Minister, International Department of the CCP Central Committee, six areas where the CCP can 'learn' from foreign political parties include—theoretical renovation, political mobilisation, decision-making processes, shaping socioeconomic development, crisis management and international public relations. The parties that find favour amongst the CCP members include Britain's Labour Party, Singapore's People's Action Party and Sweden's Social Democratic Party (Jiarui, 2005 and Brodsgaard *et al.*, 2004).

How far have Economic Reforms Transformed the CCP?

According to Dickson (2007a), 'The CCP has not been a bystander in the process of economic and social change…its policies has been the direct cause of economic growth, and the Party has embraced newly emerging economic and social elites.'

Since 1979 the CCP has been restructuring the economy with the stated objective of achieving 'socialist modernisation.' In the mid-1980s the focus shifted to the creation of a 'socialist market economy'. A fundamental challenge facing the Party is the creation of a 'market economy' that will supplant the current half measure of alternating between the plan and the market.

At the level of official political thought and social philosophy, China's reformists have managed to refrain from counterposing 'the market' and its values *versus* 'socialism', as that would unavoidably provoke a systemic choice between the two. To quote Vivienne Shue (2008):

> They (the reformers) have instead, very gradually but deliberately, worked to obscure and blur the boundaries between the two, moving to incorporate concepts and social values associated with the "market" into the official ideology of the still 'socialist' state.

The transformation of the CCP has brought about a fundamental shift in the way the Chinese state is looked at today. For Wei-Wei Zhang (2006), 'the state has gradually turned itself from an anti-market totalitarian institution into a largely pro-business authoritarian institution'—leading many to wonder and speculate whether the revolution that brought the Party to power in 1949 has become extinguished by the more alluring prospect of material progress over everything else.

The Party's membership policy during the reform era emphasises 'four transformations' *(sihua)*, i.e., 'revolutionisation' *(geminhua)*, 'juvenescence' *(nianqinhua)*, 'intellectual and educational competency' *(zhishihua)*, and 'professional competency' *(zhuanyehua)* of new members. After the 16th Party Congress, emphasis on Party members' educational and professional competencies has been modified to emphasise on 'governing ability (*zhizheng nengli*)' of the Party, that is, the ability to manage the socialist market economy, the ability to develop socialist democracy (*shehui zhuyi minzhu zhengzhi*), the ability to promote an advanced socialistic culture (*shehui zhuyi xianjin wenhua*) and the ability to build a socialistic harmonious society (*shehui zhuyi hexie shehui*) (see Sato and Eto, 2006).[1]

A looming challenge faced by the CCP is the pressure for political reform that becomes more difficult to avoid as there is indeed a visible disconnect between a market-oriented economy and a dynamic society, on the one hand, and an anachronistic and authoritarian state on the other. In order to satisfy and temper these demands the Party has initiated three broad trends—institutionalisation of the leadership system with an emphasis on normative rules and procedures; the effort to make government more accountable to an increasingly pluralistic society; and, the improvement of citizens' legal/constitutional rights (Zhao, 2006). These trends highlight the 'absorptive' tendencies of the CCP and its flexibility in adjusting to the rapidly changing realities. Reform has created 'independent sources of wealth, power and influence' that the CCP has identified as a constituency to be co-opted, lest they develop political ideas and associations of their own, and beyond the reach of the CCP (Dickson, 2007b).[2] It is argued that the system of 'multiparty cooperation and consultation' promoted by the CCP is an effort to tap into and

---

1. Author's note: The *pinyin* expressions are as they appeared in the original text (pp. 176-78).

2. The 'new elites' as a class owe their origin to the reforms and the economic success it has spawned. It is estimated that China had over 3.6 million private firms that produced more than 50 per cent of its GDP, created 57 million jobs and contributed 40 per cent of tax revenues in 2004.

accommodate 'political actors' who exist outside Party mechanisms and are representative of the churning in society influenced by the reforms (People's Daily, 2008a).

Does the CCP profess any Ideology and what are the Principle Themes the Leadership is Projecting to Retain its hold on the 'Masses'?

The functions of ideology for the CCP are twofold—first, ideology plays the role of an 'integrator', providing a basis for the coming together of diverse groups and agendas; and second, by organising and socialising members to a political culture, ideology plays the role of 'role articulation'. Since the progressive implementation of the reforms, the Party for all practical purposes has adopted an 'agnostic' approach towards ideological precepts. A visible illustration of a shift in ideological positions is seen when comparing Jiang Zemin with Hu Jintao. Jiang Zemin highlighted the need for 'political stability' while Hu Jintao has shifted the goalpost towards ensuring 'social stability'.

Hu Jintao reinterprets Jiang Zemin's 'Three Represents' as the 'Three People's Principles' namely: use my power for the people; link my feelings to the people; and, focus my heart on the pursuit of public welfare (Jintao, 2003).[3] The Hu-Wen administration realises the danger of 'social instability' arising from the social impact of the reform process and has adopted the 'putting people first' (*yiren weiben*) approach as also the 'construction of a harmonious society' (*hexie shehui*). The overriding need for 'stability' for the Party arises from several areas of concern, namely, reducing unemployment, improving social security system, increasing fiscal revenue, cutting public funding and correcting and standardising economic order.

Hu Jintao in an attempt at carving out a legacy for himself has through his tours and speeches, projected a shift in China's developmental paradigm that lays emphasis on society first. By doing so he aims to achieve the enhancement of state authority on the one hand and political

3. Also known as the 'Xin sanmin zhuyi' or the 'three new people's principles'—to use power for the people (*quan weimin shuoyong*); to link sentiments to the people (*qing weimin shuoji*); and, to pursue the interest of the people (*li weimin shuomo*).

control on the other. The concept of 'Scientific Development' ascribed to Hu Jintao is to be interpreted as an ideological approach that takes cognisance of the myriad problems facing China today that are in many ways a result of the reforms initiated three decades ago—inadequate health care, income disparities, absence of social security and looming environmental concerns to name a few. The Party has initiated programmes to promote the essence of 'scientific development' since the 17th National Congress held in 2007 incorporated the 'scientific outlook on development' into the Party constitution. The concept is promoted as a logical follow up of the thoughts on development put forward by the Party's collective leadership and is considered a Marxist outlook on the methodology of development (People's Daily Online, 2008). In keeping with the priority given by Hu Jintao to the societal concerns, he and the CCP have also introduced the theme of 'harmonious society'—that encompasses elements of fairness and uprightness, rule of law, order, democracy and the balance between the needs of man and nature, as endorsed by the 10th NPC in March 2006 (Zhengxu and Fook, 2007).

Table 2.1

Ascribed Political Values: Pre- and Post-Reform China

Pre-Reform China	*Post-Reform China*	*Ascribed Political Value*
Revolutionary fervour	Rationalisation and institutionalisation	Shift in ideological temperament
Idealism and personality cult	Pragmatism and technocracy	From 'charismatic' leadership to 'ration-legal' leadership
Class struggle	Economic development	Abandoning socialist rhetoric; adopting market incentive
Revolutionary logic	Legal code	Socialist world revolution given up in favour of rule of law
Politics in command	Social stability	Regime consolidation gives way to assuaging social concerns
Totalitarian power	Rationalisation of political power	Absolute power over all spheres gives way to a tempered exercise of power
Centralised power	Relative autonomy	Exclusive political control over economy shifts in favour of autonomous economic management

Source: See Guo (2006).

Guo's (2006) table reproduced here captures the essence of ascribed political values in China in the pre-reform and post-reform periods respectively.

What is the State of Central-Region/Local Relations?

Chinese history is replete with instances of heated debates and power struggles over '*junxianzhi*' (a unified and centralised political system with local administrative prefectures and counties) as against '*fengjianzhi*' (a decentralised enfeoffment system) (See Hao and Zhimin, 1994).[4] There is an 'unresolved historical problem of power distribution and institutionalisation within the Chinese political system' (Li, 1998). After three decades of economic reform and several phases of institutional reform, Central-local relations in China are in a continuous process of transformation. The balance of power between Centre and province is constantly fluctuating, as provincial authorities have gained resources in the reform era. The Centre exercises political sovereignty by controlling the military and by appointing or rotating the provincial leadership. The levels below the top tier are decided by the provincial leadership.

Increasing autonomy at the lower levels of the provincial administration has created conditions for the Centre to continuously adapt and modify its relations with localities. It could also be argued that to treat the Chinese state as 'absolute' and 'monolithic' is *passé*, as in many instances the directions and inspiration for economic reform is provided by provinces like Guangdong, and municipalities like Shanghai. Displaying an amazing knack of maneuvering through obstacles placed by the Central authorities, the provincial and municipal leaderships of Guangdong and Shanghai have bargained with Central leaders, to fashion policies that stimulate and attract investment.

The Central-local relationship in China is primarily agent-driven and is being shaped at the meeting point of politics and economics. The economic necessities of a locality intersect with a particular political approach to ensure its successful fruition. Local governments, especially at

4. 'Enfeoffment' refers to land deeds given to individuals with caveats—primarily regarding the duration, as according to law all land in China belongs to the state.

the county and township levels have been the key players facilitating China's transition to a capitalist economy. It is at these levels that market entrepreneurialism has succeeded (Caulfield, 2006). The repeated waves of decentralisation launched by the Centre since the reforms commenced in 1979 have occurred 'as a systematic response by the provinces to changes in the constraints imposed by the political centre in Beijing and by provincial agents' (Krug, 2002). It would appear that Central control, enforced from the top, was operated through the system of work units, personnel management, employment, household registration, health care etc. Three significant developments that have taken place and have a bearing on Central-local relations are: first, in the reform period, significant shifts of control over national resources has taken place from Central to local governments; second, local authorities do contest the Central authority in ensuring policy implementation; and third, the Centre is increasingly encouraging initiation of policy at the local level. These are indications of the emergence of a negotiated Centre-region/local relationship. To quote Zhao Suisheng (1994):

> ...progressive decentralisation has undercut the efficacy of the central authority's coercive instruments and undermined the centre's capacity to enforce compliance from local governments.

One of the most important issues influencing relations between the Central government in Beijing and the provincial governments is that of land. The debates, proposals, and laws passed on land use have a far reaching impact on society. For provincial and local governments, land is the primary source of wealth and government patronage. With decentralisation in attracting development related investment, local authorities in provinces compete with each other to offer land on attractive terms (sometimes free!) to developers and investors. As a consequence, this 'competition' for allocating land for 'development' (factories, residential housing etc.) has led to millions of families and thousands of villages being uprooted from their original places of residence, and has also exposed the need for the Central government to 're-look' into the question of land reforms. An examination of the need for land reforms was also prompted by the striking income inequalities between rural and urban residents (Li, 2009). From a society that was more or less equal in the early 1980s, the reform process of urban areas since the last two decades has led to wide income disparities. This is the proximate reason for the Hu-Wen combine emphasising their 'social approach' and concern for ordinary people.[5] In October 2008, the CCP passed the 'Resolution of the CCP Central Committee on Some Major Issues in Rural Reform and Development' approving plans for newer land reform with twin objectives—increase agricultural productivity and increase the rural resident's income. Successive programmes for institutionalisation have influenced the working of Centre-province relations. The Centre and the provinces are, in principle, allies in the task of administering the country and enforcing the 'rule of law'. The logical outcome of the processes is the identifying and demarcation of 'jurisdiction'. The three decades of reform in China have thus grafted new concepts onto the political lexicon describing Centre-province relations as being guided by 'interdependency', 'indispensability', 'accommodation' and 'compromise'.[6]

Does the CCP Consider itself 'An Agent of Change'?

The CCP does take its role seriously as a harbinger of change. After three decades of reform, the approach to the political class is now conditioned by the 'realisation' that a market economy is pronouncedly more productive than a planned economy. Three decades of reform have witnessed the transformation of China from a totalitarian state to an authoritarian one that holds a monopoly of power through the alliances it has forged among the elites—the CCP, economic managers, new entrepreneurs and a substantial sector of the intelligentsia (Xiaoguang, 2006). Changes in organisation and ideology have led to greater space for political engagement by different social groups. The CCP is averse to bottom-up initiatives; it is more amenable to a top-down approach, so as to maintain control on developments.

---

5. Hu has raised the 'new three principles of people' (*xin sanminzhuyi*)—i.e., 'power must be used for the people, (cadres') sentiments must be tied to those of the people, and material benefits must be sought in the interests of the people.' Hu's 'principles' provide an interesting contrast to his predecessor Jiang Zemin's 'Three Represents' (*sangge daibiao*)—the 'Three Represents' state that the CCP must always represent: 'the development trend of China's advanced productive forces; the orientation of China's advanced culture; and, the fundamental interests of the overwhelming majority of the people.'

6. See Li (1998): 287.

If the CCP desires to act as a 'ruling Party' or 'governing Party' as opposed to its 'revolutionary heritage', it needs to create a system of governing the country through law and a legal-rational bureaucracy and resist the temptation of trying to control those forums that have emerged outside Party control in the reform years. As Joseph Fewsmith has pointed out, 'to exercise political control as a ruling Party the CCP needs to move away from the traditional model of controlling society through the penetration of *danwei* (work units) and exercise control geographically through the use of law' (Fewsmith, 2006: 42).

The efforts by the CCP have generated expectations that as the reform process moves onto the next phase of 'deep reform', the CCP itself will transform its very identity. The inclusion of corporatist members within the CCP is characteristic of a system identifying a rationale to connect state and society (Unger and Chan, 1995). By maintaining its core agenda of economic reform, the Chinese political system opens up new spaces for political participation. The obverse of this positive feature is a dire need on the part of the CCP to address growing contradictions manifesting themselves throughout China. For noted dissident Liu Xiaobo, there are four contradictions dominating China today—first, the contradiction between the 'market economy' and system of 'official monopoly'; second, the contradiction between 'privatisation' and the pursuit of 'efficiency and social justice'; third, the contradiction between a 'fast growing economy' and 'faster growing corruption'; and, fourth, the contradiction between the 'monolithism' of the political regime and the 'pluralisation of society'(Xiaobo, 2006).

Is the CCP's Legitimacy Under Threat?

As Lipset (1981) put it, Legitimacy is 'the capacity of the system to engender and maintain the belief that the existing political institutions are the most appropriate ones for society.'

Legitimacy in socialist states is rooted, in an ideational culture, constituted by a dominant mode of communication that is identical to the (surrounding) symbolic environment. To structure a conducive political environment, a state needs to merely manipulate its citizens to accept the prevalent political order as legitimate by controlling its mass media (Lynch, 1999). The CCP with its vast propaganda machinery does just that.

For more than three decades until the reforms of 1978, 'revolution' itself was the primary criteria adopted by the CCP to claim legitimacy. With the reforms fast becoming an irreversible process, the CCP has constantly proclaimed its desire to create 'the rule of law' as the primary governing instrument and hence legitimacy. In the words of Pittman B. Potter (1994), 'by relying on the socialist legal system as a source of legitimacy, the regime also strengthens its ability to justify specific actions by reference to law'. The CCP realises that legitimacy and governance require a legal and constitutional foundation (Dittmer and Liu, 2006). 'Legitimacy' for the CCP derives from the creation of institutions securing consent and mobilising resources in meeting popular expectations (Hay, 2006). The manner in which 'procedural authority' and the 'rule of law' are becoming sacrosanct for the political elite, it recalls the emphasis on 'institutional power' and 'rational-legal forms of authority' which is a prominent theme in Max Weber's writings. This implies office holders displaying merits accrued from exposure to 'formal training' and the importance of career distinction (Kratochwil, 2006). The above virtues support Fei Ling Wang's assertion that the post Mao state has sought legitimacy through 'bureaucratic efficiency' and an emphasis on 'modernisation values' (Wang, 1998). A different interpretation of the CCP's approach to 'legitimacy' and the CCP comes from Huang and Yang (2002), who feel that the Chinese state is representing legitimacy by shifting contentious political issues into the administrative 'neutral' zone, where professional and non-coercive institutions lie.

In an attempt to create an ideological premise that satisfies the new realities of a transitional economy, the lifting of the ban on entrepreneurs joining the Party, as indicated in the 'Three Represents' was an attempt by the CCP to further legitimise itself by incorporating a section of society whose very success was based on the Party having created space for incremental change. The Party was apprehensive that not co-opting this section of society could leave open a residual possibility of internal subversion or opposition. Wang Changjiang of the Central Party School—the crucible for Party leadership in China—argued that, if the Party did not embrace the vast majority of the Chinese people, they would seek to organise themselves outside the political system (Fewsmith, 2006: 88).

A severe test for the legitimacy of the Party is to be found in the growing number of 'collective incidents'—the euphemism for popular protests. The increase in the number of such incidents, from 8,706 reported in 1993 to 87,000 reported incidents in 2005, is seen by the Party as a serious problem threatening social stability and, consequently, the legitimacy of the Party's rule in rural areas. The issues that mobilise collective grievances in the countryside include land expropriation, rampant cadre corruption, rigged village elections, government violence against protesting villagers, excessive local taxation (ameliorated no doubt by the progressive abolition of agricultural taxes since 2004), pollution of farmland and drinking water, illegal mining (with frequent loss of life), the birth control policy, the household registration system and the systematic discrimination against rural dwellers in education, medical care and social welfare (Lianjiang, 2006).

The CCP is actively promoting itself as the 'governing Party'. It was in 2004, the 'CCP acknowledged for the first time, that the 1949 revolution no longer served as a durable basis for legitimacy', (Gilley, 2008). For Gilley 'regime survival in China is dependent on a combination of authoritarian-supporting modernist values and legitimacy-enhancing "contained" institutional change.'[7] 'Legitimacy' for the CCP derives from meeting popular expectations and from the creation of institutions that secure consent, and mobilise resources. The CCP strives to ensure that its legitimacy is enforced through procedural mechanisms at the political level. A few features include: a relatively smooth leadership transition; institutionalisation of political elite selection for important positions within the Party and the government; further separation of political and administrative functions of the Party-state; a gradual expansion of the political discourse; the conduct of village elections and self-governance experiments in residential communities; and, a constant reformulation of official ideology. Hu Jintao has channelised his energies towards continuing the process of rationalisation by focussing on developing rules, norms, procedures and institutions to codify the policy breakthroughs thereby

7. Ibid.: 277.

lending gravity to ensure procedural legitimacy. The annual sessions of the 11th National People's Congress (NPC) and the 11th China People's Political Consultative Conference (CPPCC) held in March 2009 are to be seen as efforts in this direction. These sessions discussed at length plans for further institutional reform of the government (Poeple's Daily, 2008b).

Conclusion

In conclusion, the CCP can rightly lay claim to having initiated the economic reform programme that has not only made China a workshop for the rest of the world, but has also to a large extent 'liberated' its citizens in the economic sphere. Now that after three decades of economic reform since 1979, questions are being raised on the need for political reform as well, the CCP's response has been to ensure control and regulate the processes of change so as to ensure overall stability. This includes the initiating and conduct of public debate in a guided manner on selected issues such as the need for the 'rule of law' and 'good governance'—which does not involve the danger of rocking the boat.

The task before the CCP is to translate the visible successes achieved in the economic sphere to the political realm. This is a deeply contested endeavour that involves several fundamental choices to be made. First, unless basic changes are carried out in the CCP's foundational ideology and structure, there cannot be any significant demonstration effect in the political realm. Second, the process of transforming the Party from its revolutionary ethos to a governing entity is no easy task, as ideological shifts and political compromises which are perfectly rational and justifiable have to be made. Third, for a large developing country like China, to move out of a political culture that is authoritarian to one which permits greater competition among different players is a task that China has no model to learn from and, last, are China and the CCP ready for all of the above?

References

Brodsgaard, Kjeld Erik and Zheng Yongnian (eds.) (2004). *Bringing the Party Back In: How China is Governed.* Singapore: Eastern University Press.

Caulfield, Janice L. (2006). "Local Government Reform in China: A Rational Actor Perspective", *International Review of Administrative Sciences* 72(2): 253. June. Brussels, IIAS: Sage.

Dickson, Bruce J. (2007a). "The Party is Far From Over", *Current History* 107(701): 243. Philadelphia, PA.

———. (2007b). "Integrating Wealth and Power in China: The Communist Party's Embrace of the Private Sector", *The China Quarterly* 192: 827-54. December.

———. (2006a). "Who does the Party Represent?: From 'Three Revolutionary Classes' to 'Three Represents'", in Tun-jen Cheng, Jaques deLisle and Deborah Brown (eds.), *China Under Hu Jintao—Opportunities, Dangers and Dilemmas*, Series on Contemporary China, 2: 75-97. Singapore: World Scientific.

———. (2006b). "Cooptation and Corporatism in China: The Logic of Party Adaptation", in Lowell Dittmer and Guoli Liu (eds.), *China's Deep Reform—Domestic Politics in Transition.* Lanham, MD: Rowman & Littlefield. pp. 119-124.

———. (2003). *Red Capitalists in China: The Party, Private Entrepreneurs and Prospects for Political Change.* New York: Cambridge University Press.

Dittmer, Lowell and Guoli Liu (eds.) (2006). *China's Deep Reform—Domestic Politics in Transition.* Lanham, MD: Rowman & Littlefield. pp. 1-24.

Fewsmith, Joseph (2006). "Political Succession: Changing Guards and Changing Rules", in Tun-jen Cheng, Jaques deLisle and Deborah Brown (eds.), *China Under Hu Jintao—Opportunities, Dangers and Dilemmas*, Series on Contemporary China—Vol. 2. Singapore: World Scientific. p.42, 88.

Gilley, Bruce (2008). "Legitimacy and Institutional Change—The Case of China", *Comparative Political Studies* 41(3): 269. Thousand Oaks. March.

Goodman, David S.G. (ed.) (2008). *The New Rich in China—Future Rulers, Present Lives.* Abingdon: Routledge. p.36.

Guo, Baogang (2006). "Political Legitimacy in China's Transition Toward a Market Economy", in Lowell Dittmer and Guoli Liu (eds.), *China's Deep Reform—Domestic Politics in Transition.* Lanham, MD: Rowman & Littlefield.

Hao, Jia and Lin Zhimin (eds.) (1994). *Changing Central-Local Relations in China—Reforms and State Capacity.* Boulder, CO: Westview Press. p.1.

Hay, William Anthony (2006). "What is Democracy? Liberal Institutions and Stability in Changing Societies", FPRI Study Group on *America and the West* 50(1). Orbis Philadelphia, PA. Winter.

Huang, Yanzhong and Dali Yang (2002). "Bureaucratic Capacity and State-Society Relations in China", *Journal of Chinese Political Science* 7(1&2): 19-46. Springer. March.

Jiarui, Wang (2005). *Waiguo zhengdang de zhizheng jingyan jiaoxun* (Expereince and Lessons of the Foreign Ruling Parties) *Xuexi Yu Cankao* (Study and Reference) No. 2, pp. 7-13 as cited in Wei-Wei Zhang (2006). "Long-Term Outlook for China's Political Reform", *Asia-Europe Journal* 4(2): 157, Heidelberg, June.

Jintao, Hu (2003). "Speech at the Graduation Ceremony of the Seminar on the Theory of the Three Represents", *People's Daily,* 18 February.

Katz, Richard S. and William Crotty (eds.) (2006). *Handbook of Party Politics.* London: Sage. p.473.

Kratochwil, Friedrich (2006). "On Legitimacy", *International Relations* 20(3): 306. Aberystwyth, Wales. September.

Krug, Barbara (2002). "Why Provinces?", in John Fitzgerald (ed.), *Rethinking China's Provinces.* London: Routledge. p. 263.

Li, Cheng (2009). "Hu Jintao's Land Reform: Ambition, Ambiguity and Anxiety", *China Leadership Monitor* 27, Washington: Hoover Institution. Winter.

Li, Linda Chelan (1998). *Centre and Provinces—China 1978-1993—Power as Non-Zero Sum Game.* Oxford: Clarendon Press. p.2.

Lianjiang, Li (2006). "Driven to Protest: China's Rural Unrest", *Current History* 105(692): 252. September. Philadelphia.

Lipset, Seymour Martin (1981). *Political Man.* Baltimore: Johns Hopkins University Press. p.64.

Lynch, Daniel C. (1999). *After the Propaganda State—Media, Politics, and "Thought Work" in Reformed China.* Stanford: Stanford University Press. p.2.

People's Daily (2008a). "Cause of Multi-Party Cooperation Promising", 26 February. Accessible at: *http://english.people.com.cn/90001/90780/91342/6361131.html* (Accessed on 26 October 2008).

———. (2008b) "Why 2008 NPC, CPPCC Sessions are so Conspicuous?", 4 March 2008, Beijing. Accessible at: *http://english.peopledaily.com.cn/90001/90780/91342/6366024.html* (Accessed on 30 October 2008).

People's Daily Online (2008). "CPC Launches Pilot Program to Promote Scientific Development", *People's Daily Online*, Beijing, 16 April. Accessible at: *http://english.peopledaily.com. cn/90002/91580/91598/6504430.html* (Accessed on 30 October 2008).

Potter, Pittman B. (1994). "Riding the Tiger: Legitimacy and Legal Structure in Post-Mao China", *The China Quarterly* (138): 325. June.

Sartori, G. (1996). *Parties and Party Systems: A Framework of Analysis.* Cambridge: Cambridge University Press.

Sato, Hiroshi and Keiya Eto (2006). "Party Membership in Post-reform China: Age, Educational Attainment, and Professional Competency", Ch. 9 in Nakajone Katsuji and Kojima Tomoyuki (ed.), *Restructuring China—Party, State and Society after the Reform and Open Door.* Tokyo: Toyo Bunko. pp. 176-203.

Shue, Vivienne (2008). "Rule as Repertory and the Compound Essence of Authority", *Modern China* 34(1): 145. January. Thousand Oaks, CA.

Suisheng, Zhao (1994). "China's Central-Local Relationship: A Historical Perspective", in Jia Hao and Lin Zhimin (eds.), *Changing Central-Local Relations in China—Reforms and State Capacity.* Boulder, CO: Westview Press. p. 29.

Unger, Jonathan and Anita Chan (1995). "Corporatism in China: A Developmental State in an East Asian Context", in Barrett L. McCormick and Jonathan Unger (eds.), *China after Socialism: In the Footsteps of Eastern Europe or East Asia*?. Armonk, NY: M.E. Sharpe. p.111.

Wang, Fei Ling (1998). *Institutions and Institutional Change in China: Premodernity and Modernization.* New York: St. Martin's.

Ware, Alan (1996). *Political Parties and Party Systems.* Oxford: Oxford University Press.

Xiaobo, Liu (2006). "Reform in China: The Role of Civil Society", *Social Research* 73(1): 123. New York. Spring.

Xiaoguang, Kang (2006). "Confucianization: A Future in the Tradition", *Social Research* 73(1): 77-120. Spring. New York.

Zhang, Wei-Wei (2006). "Long-term Outlook for China's Political Reform", *Asia-Europe Journal* 4(2): 157, June. Heidelberg.

Zhao, Suisheng (ed.) (2006). *Debating Political Reform in China—Rule of Law vs. Democratization*. New York: M.E. Sharpe. p.xiv.

Zhengxu, Wang and Lye Liang Fook (2007). "Responding to Challenges and Problems of Governance", in Wang Gungwu and John Wong (eds.), *Interpreting China's Development*. Singapore: World Scientific. pp.3-10.

3 China's Internal Contradictions

A Sociopolitical Analysis

Ravni Thakur

> Mechanical and superficial views still boast empirical and ideological clarity, yet they invariably depend on obsolete binary opposites—state *vs.* society, official *vs.* unofficial, and dictatorship *vs.* democracy
>
> —Xudong Zhang (2001)

Introduction

China today is a country that cannot be simply classified according to the old frameworks within which it has been approached till now. Western scholars of China have always tended to view and try to understand China through the limited framework that Xu criticises in the quotation above. Such 'mechanical and superficial' understandings more often than not fail to see the new forms of material power distribution, social representation and ideological contradictions. China represents a complicated plurality dominated by a new socioeconomic polity. It is not a unitary society, but one that is beset with differences and contradictions that have huge implications for the future of the country and its internal organisation. These differences and competing discourses of legitimacy exist at different levels in the body politic of China. My forthcoming book on social stratification in China, talks of the various reasons that cause this stratification. This paper is the summary of the book.

Several changes since the 1980s and, more markedly, since the turn of the century have today coalesced to create a new reality of power and control in China. It is well known that since the economic reforms were put into effect, Chinese society as a whole has become increasingly stratified. This has meant that, till recently, instead of creating a strong, united society based on class solidarity, new discourses of nation building and loyalty emerged. What came into prominence was the Confucian concept of 'harmonious society', premised on shared nationalism and ethnic Han homogeneity—the latter being a throw back to the glories of the Ming Empire, in which the Han was the dominant race. But now, signs of change are visible in various areas. The first is the discourse within the Party about its ideology and the role it needs to play. The second is the role played by education towards cementing social stratification in China. Finally, if what we are seeing in China can be called the emergence of a new class, the question one asks is: is the socioeconomic revolution leading to the re-emergence of a capitalist class? If so, who does it consist of? Is there an identifiable capitalist class and a middle class in China? However, this new concept of reality is not going uncontested in the country. It is a subject of heated debates in the Party and academia.

The repositioning of the Party at ideological levels and the debates thereof are intrinsic to an understanding of the different layers of social stratification or, to invoke Bourdieu (1987), the differences/distinctions, that one sees in China today. The purpose of this paper is to move away from stereotyping the Chinese society, while at the same time attempting to grasp the embryonic contradictions that exist within its society—contradictions that, taken to their logical conclusion, could well undermine the stability of the country and force the Chinese Communist Party (CCP) into a corner.

I

Ideological and Intellectual Level

The last few years have seen the publication of several books that have pointed out the internal problems that beset China today. Susan Shirk's book, *China: Fragile Superpower* (2007), is only one in a long list of such books. While I do not agree entirely with Shirk, my contention is that the comparative openness of Chinese society today, the rise of intellectual think tanks and their contacts with the West and, above all, the emergence of China as a class stratified society, has created inevitable contradictions between the existing reality and the ideology professed by the CCP. The first major change at the ideological level is within the Party itself. The CCP is today trying to play a centralist role between different schools of opinion among the intellectual think tanks, but it has changed at all levels, throwing up new opposing elements that are reflected in the new dynamics of a stratified society. Since the 1990s, the Party too has changed radically in character and become a technocratic entity with younger and more qualified people. Sato and Eto (2008) in an article on 'The Changing Structure of Communist Party Membership', point out how, since the 1990s, the Party has outlined four criteria or four transformations for Party membership, they being: (1) revolutionised (*geminghua*), (2) younger (*nianqing hua*), (3) intellectual and well educated (*zhishi hua*), and (4) professionalised (*zhuanye hua*). This change coincided with Jiang Zemin's agenda to make the Party more inclusive and broaden its reach to include those previously defined as class enemies. Thus the Party has changed both in ideology and in practice—i.e., recruitment of cadre, resource and criteria for Party membership. This is both reflective of social tension and social stratification that is emerging in China. Socially stratified education is playing a fundamental role in generational and regional divides and, as is the case elsewhere in the world, becoming a purveyor of distinction, an issue which will be taken up later.

Along with its criteria for membership, the Party took the lead in redefining the aim of China's development strategy from socialist modernisation to a socialist market economy. This emphasis on 'market economy' has created, for the first time, serious contradictions at the intellectual level. The joke in China today is a pun on the word '*qian*'—which means both the future and money, even though the characters are different. *Xiang qian kan*, they say, no longer means look to the future but look to money! This kind of thinking shows the pervasiveness of the belief that the Chinese society is a capitalist society led by a CCP that still supposedly rules in the name of the working class. A quick look at the distribution of Party membership among private entrepreneurs makes for an interesting reading. Jie and Dickson differentiate between red capitalists—i.e., those who were already members of the Party and/or ran state-owned enterprises (SOEs) before being classified as entrepreneurs—and those who have joined the Party after being classified as entrepreneurs. Out of the total of 2,048 members they interviewed, eight per cent are red capitalists and the rest were those who became members after classification.

In field work that was carried out in China in 2006 amongst students of three prestigious universities, Chengdu, Yunnan and Beijing, it was noted that membership of the Party was crucial for serious upward mobility and provided stability no matter what one did. Out of the 150 students interviewed, everyone had applied for membership and 64 were already members. The result of this changed recruitment criteria has meant, that the Party as such has become middle class in nature, just as higher education has. Educational criteria remain extremely important for membership. This 'middle-classing' of the Party has provided the Party with broad support within urban China and amongst the educated elite. At the same time, the Party has disenchanted and disillusioned the very constituents it traditionally empowered—the peasants and the working classes. Amongst them, the Party is 'corrupt and capitalist'. And field work shows that what we see is the emergence of what Solinger calls 'cadre merchant', Y So calls 'embourgeoisement', and others 'state capitalism', 'clientele capitalism', etc. It is the Party that is the patron, thus still maintaining that vertical hierarchy, *albeit* through different means and tools. It is this merchant-bureaucrat embedded network that is today seen as the economic and political oppressor. This also means that the anger born of class contradictions is directed at the state. The state, instead of being a mediator in class conflicts, becomes the source of conflict. This is the first fault line and the internal contradiction in China today.

An emphasis on educational qualifications automatically implies that a large population of workers and peasants, who only make it through the compulsory nine years of education—and in rural areas, some not even that—automatically lose out on membership. Access to education, especially higher education, is thus becoming a major point of social stratification. This will be discussed in Part II of the paper.

It is these redefinitions that have led to extensive debate amongst the intelligentsia, on both development policy planning, as well as on how far China should turn into a genuine market economy. This debate deals both with ideology and economic planning. The first is part of the great reform economics that was spearheaded by Deng Xiaoping. These ideologues categorically support the reform process and have manned the state's think tanks, especially under Jiang Zemin. The main thrust of their argument remains grounded in market economics—globalisation taken as the decentralisation of economic planning. The second group, that can be described as university intellectuals, writers and members of civil society, are not opposed to reform, but have launched an ideological attack from a 'new left' perspective. This group has concentrated on the negative fallout of the economic reforms process, which widens the economic and social divide in China. A second cleavage between the left and the reformists is the left's push for liberal democracy both within the Party and in the civil society.

Scholars such as Xudong Zhang, Wang Hui and members of the Sociology departments and Chinese Academy of Social Sciences (CASS) departments represent the 'new left' critique and scholars like Li Peilin etc., are its leading lights. They have collected extensive field work data documenting income and educational disparities in China today. First, authors like Wang Hui who was the editor of the journal *Dushu* provide theoretical critique of the process of globalisation and neo-liberal economic paradigms. Wang Hui (2001) makes the point when he says:

> China's continued support for socialism poses no obstacle to the following conclusion: In all its behaviours, including economic, political and cultural—even in government behaviour—China has completely conformed to the dictates of capital and activities of the market.

What is of deep concern to Wang Hui and the other scholars is the social processes unleashed by a capitalist market economy and a virtual capitalist state in the guise of a Socialist state. They go on to attack the commercialisation of society and accuse the state of being the handmaiden of global capital. Their criticism is that Chinese intellectuals who have bought into the ideology of globalisation have either turned to tradition, such as Confucianism, or have propagated the theory of the rise of Asian capitalism and China's important role in this rise. The nationalist desire for super power status also comes in for criticism. Shaoguang Wang, for example, reiterates that such extraneous issues should not make the state deviate from its main task, which was and is the welfare of the common man and the policies thereof. Criticising those who advocate a strengthening of the market economy and a greater retreat of the state from the field, he argues: 'Some people believe that once the stifling state is knocked out of the economic realm, market forces would emerge full blown to put human society in perfect order'. This, he goes on to argue, is 'the most dangerous of illusions.'[1] Thus we find in the new left a powerful theoretical opponent of the current economic and global strategies. This critique is extended to all aspects of contemporary Chinese society, to the commercialisation of its culture, the rise of conservative politics and at traditional discourses that have re-emerged after years of authoritarianism.

This critique of the growing inequalities in society has been further corroborated by excellent research carried out by social scientists in CAAS and in other departments of the Social Sciences. The *2005 Blue Book of Sociology*, is a fine example of the attention being paid to this issue.

The 'discourse of democracy' in the Party is also worth commenting on. In the post Tiananmen society, the demand for democracy does not come from society as a whole but from within the Party. I know from interaction with Party members that today there is a great deal of discussion about these issues going on within the Party. A good example of this is the kind of curriculum and books available in Party schools which are attended by a substantial number of cadre students. Studies show that today, the issue is not how 'Red' one's class background is, but how 'loyal' one is to the Party and its goals. So, one gets Party acceptance by subscribing to China's economic modernisation, but need not necessarily support a single Party state. There are people within the Party intelligentsia who believe that, along with a liberal economy, a liberal democracy should also play a role in national politics. The 1980s saw a call for democracy within a Marxian paradigm, with intellectuals like Su Shaozhi, Wang Ruoshui etc., asking for 'socialist democracy and legal rights for citizens'. Today, it is people like Li Shenzhi, former Vice-President of CASS and a former Vice-Minister, who is the leading voice of change, the voice of liberalism. Feng Chongyi (2008), in an excellent article quotes Li as saying in a book in 1988:

> After three hundred years of comparison and selection in the whole world since the age of industrialisation, and particularly after one hundred years of Chinese experimentation, one of the largest in the scale of human history, there is sufficient evidence to prove that liberalism is the best human value.

1. Ibid.: Hui: 207-08.

This is corroborated by interviews with students, those able to and willing to aspire to the middle class and middle class liberalism. This younger generation also saw middle class values as including multi-plurality. Feng goes on to quote another senior, Du Guang, former head of the Party school, who wrote a long article on Party authoritarianism or communist despotism. This article even went as far as to ask for the army to be separated from the Party, and grant independence to trade unions.

All these critiques are based on the perception that the ruling Party is pursuing an ideologically contradictory agenda. For example, within the Party, the CCP has already set in place a more democratic agenda. The General Secretary does not get more than two terms and Deng's big contribution to democracy has been to fix the terms for all members of leading bodies within the Party, the Politburo, and the NPC. This is the present CCP's leadership's negation of Maoist totalitarianism. Despite such measures, the Party remains authoritarian as far as the '*aam adami* of China' (common man) is concerned. The CCP and its supporters appear to be caught in a time warp. They are competing with the internet, sms, etc., in the game of exercising control. They have a hundred thousand employees surfing the internet every day, exhibiting the paranoid spying habit of all totalitarian regimes, not just Marxist. It is today a totalitarian as well as a rich capitalist Party, which draws its support from a middle class and the class of private entrepreneurs. It also seeks its support, like capitalist totalitarian regimes across the world, from an embedded middle class and the beneficiaries of economic reform and, above all, total support of the People's Liberation Army (PLA). The Party stands as a representative of a capitalist state. It is no more the representative of the working class, the peasantry or the hordes of migrant labour.

This is a pervasive grudge among the common people: a cross-section of people sharing this sentiment. For them, the Party now represents big business, corruption and a lack of concern for the masses outside its charmed circle. Wanli Zhang's article (2002: 49) in the special issue of the Social Science Academy looks closely at the way the market economy has influenced the social structure in China and resulted in changes in the allocation of resources. He sees three major elements that typify this change: (1) possession and redistribution of power, (2) the emergence of free flowing resources and free space outside the old system, (3) evolution of social relationships from universalism (everyone was once comrade) to utility oriented relationships. He contends that the power delegation relationship led by the CCP will no longer dominate the social landscape, although it will remain dominant. Here the emergence of a vibrant and free commodity exchange market will determine the relationship between various social groups. Going by the three basic changes he has identified, Zhang lists five major interest groups within urban China today. Broadly, these are workers, peasants, cadres, intellectuals/white collar service sector and private business owners. Thus, market reform and the greater freedom in terms of access to resources and a say in decision-making is seen as the fundamental impetus for the emerging social differentiation process in China.

II

The Dynamics of Social Stratification

At the theoretical level, this paper raises questions on how one can identify the practices of social stratification and the inequalities that it brings about, as also whether using the the word 'class'—with all its historical sociopolitical connotations of a socialist past—today remains appropriate as a criterion of social stratification. This issue has been well discussed by scholars like Kornai and Paulowski, who have looked at post Socialist societies in Eastern Europe. Kornai speaks of communist societies creating vertical dependencies linked to a system of patronage represented by the Party.

Sun Liping (2002), speaking about China, hits the nail on the head when he points out: 'The possession and redistribution of power relating to social resources characterised the pre-reform Party structure of social interests.' Till the reforms came, there was hardly any differentiation in Chinese society based on wealth. Riskin (1987: 89), for example, points out that until 1981, the gini-coefficient was as low as 0.16. Other studies have pointed out that in terms of income differentiation, the span ranged from 30 to 560 yuan among government cadres and an official guideline set a ratio of 6:1 for top and bottom wages in all enterprises. Amongst the rural population, around 60 per cent were classified as middle peasants. Of course, the elite with their privileged Party status was out of the purview of the classical definition of inequality. Today the situation is radically different. In 2000 the gini coefficient stood at 0.458, clearly showing the stark inequalities that have come into existence (Liping, 1996). These are the macro indicators of growing social income inequalities and, without doubt, point to a definitely emerging social stratification.

Today the road to upward social mobility is education and the inequalities in the opportunies to get that education has become the root cause of social stratification. Once he embarked on economic reform, Deng Xiaoping put an end to the politicisation of education in China. Educational policies, especially since the late 1980s, were designed to create an educated labour force that would fit into China's overall economic modernisation drive. The goal was to increase productivity and social mobility. The Minister for Education said in a recently published book (Ji, 2005): 'If China is to sustain its economic development and growth...education is the essential tool to help achieve this goal and transform its huge population into a resource.'

The law in China gives each level of government its own educational jurisdiction. The local people's government administers education at the secondary and primary school level. The access to resources and amenities is determined by two factors: regional—both rural and urban inequalities—and the private and public sectors. Overall, the Central government has left the requirements of compulsory education to local levels. It has largely stopped funding this sector and the onus now lies on regional governments. In terms of percentage of per capita, Central government investment has never been more than 2.4 per cent and this figure ranks China 114 on a global scale. Basic education is thus the responsibility of the local governments and so is the mobilisation of sources. Here again, several studies, such as that by Xuelan Rong show that poorer counties tend to spend less on this sector. They point out that one-third of the educational funds come from provincial governments, one-third from local and poorer localities which tend to cut down on the allocation. Thus, per capita expenditure per child can vary from 2,786 yuan per annum in richer east coast regions to 422 yuan in the poor western provinces of Guizhou or Gansu.

Education in China is no longer free and the costs involved are highly discouraging for the students' parents. According to their income, they have to decide whether to send their children to private or state schools, or just the ordinary ones. The quality of teachers, access to educational aids and the social capital enjoyed by different schools, thus varies widely. The notion of free schooling is a myth! Pupils have to buy their own books and stationary, payments are demanded for school buildings and sometimes, communities have to even pool in for paying teachers' salaries. The government is also encouraging foreign universities, foreign funds and private education. It has introduced community funding and asked industrial enterprises to help in setting up special schools. Today private school education has become an important criteria of upward mobility, both for income and social status. Private education, by its very nature, is the cutting edge of socioeconomic divide and it is doing its work very effectively. 'Key schools' are differently—but equally—privileged institutions run by the government, on which it spends 80 per cent of the allocated funds. They make up 20 per cent of primary and elementary schools. They are called *Zhangxin xiao xue*. They get the best teachers, students, facilities and administrators. The competition here is fierce and Party membership is of significant advantage, especially for the children of senior Party cadres. Private schools are expensive and, as in India, it is the preserve of the emerging rich in urban areas. Fees can vary from 5,000 yuan per annum to 21,000 yuan.

The basic divide and the source of economic social inequality in China was the *hukou* or residence system. This permit not only gave urban residents access to all the facilities available, but also ensured that the rural population remained confined to the countryside. Education in these areas was limited to basic literacy or primary education—i.e., the three R's,—and this too varied from region to region. Rural education has suffered greatly in the post reform era for two main reasons. First, the change in the financial structure, puts the onus for funding primary and secondary education on the counties (provincial governments), which passes it on to the generally fund crunched village councils. (Primary education is the worst hit.) The second negative effect on education has been the large scale migration of labour. These migrants have no option but to leave their children behind in the care of mostly illiterate grandparents, who can hardly be expected to care about sending the children to schools. More than half the children drop out either during or after primary school. This is symptomatic of the abysmal regional divide that is ever widening in China. Basic salaries for uneducated unskilled labour, domestic and service based, is 500-700 yuan per month.

All these elements have contributed to the increasing social stratification in China today. Disparities in the access to quality education have been the nursery of the growing societal divide, even before. Post reforms, various kinds of state institutions, including 'key schools' in the state sector provided 'quality education' and one of the main access routes was Party membership. Here again, the great divide was between the urban and the rural—more so between rich counties in the coastal region and poor counties in minority areas and in the interiors of Anhui, Jiangsu and Guizhou. Today, access to education is closely tied to occupation, income and Party membership. How are these status groups being defined and understood? And how is social stratification being analysed? Further, does the state at all have policy responses to this emerging stratification? The next section will corroborate the fact that China is emerging as a class society—as opposed to 'socialist classless' society—and the concern over internal contradictions at the social and economic levels is being voiced at the intellectual level.

The *Blue Book of Sociology*, (2002) lists 10 major clearly identifiable 'status' groups. The main study that looks at the different segments of society in China today is by Li Chunling and his team from the Social Science Academy. They identify 10 major social segments that can be seen in China today (Li and Guangjin, 2002). At the theoretical level, one notices an absolute refusal to look at these social segments emerging as 'classes'. The terminology in Western sociological studies, which goes by the differences in terms of income, education etc., are preferred to the socialistic term 'class origin'. In a way, this is appropriate because these groups still do not identify with a cohesive class interest. At present, the groups are fluid and not yet generational in nature. The groups are:

1. State and social bureaucracy: This group consists of Party cadres and administrators at all social levels. They are seen as the group that pushes through economic reforms, and is still responsible for decision-making at all levels, from the Centre to the counties and to villages. They make up 2.1 per cent of the total working population—in cities 1-5 per cent and in rural areas 0.5 per cent.[2] Li Qiang (2002), concludes that the major changes that have occurred in the profile of this section are threefold: (i)

2. Ibid.: Li and Guangjin (2002): 117.

their number has increased, (ii) the average age has fallen and (iii) they have markedly better cultural and educational backgrounds.

Researchers have been looking at how the power, originally held by this group by virtue of its total control over the distribution of sources, has been affected by the shift to market economy. Sun Liping (2002: 36) points out that, 'In the transition towards market economy, the redistributioneers (the erstwhile power elite) cannot become rich by only relying on their political stock-in-trade.' In the past, becoming a Party member was the only way to join the elite group. Today, however, one can become a member of the elite group through economic success. Thus, money is becoming a criteria for elite status.

2. Economic managers *(jingli renyuan ceng)*: This class consists of both those who manage private enterprises and those who manage state enterprises. The origins of this section is threefold. First, those who managed state or collective enterprises. Second, those who have emerged from the private sector and from technical and management trained backgrounds. They are responsible for introducing modern management techniques. Third, financial consultants and managers.

This is mainly an urban based group with good educational and specialised backgrounds. This is an important and powerful section and stands at 1.5 per cent of the urban working population.[3]

3. Private entrepreneurs: This is the newest group to emerge in China and owes its existence solely to economic reforms. Li Chunling describes these entrepreneurs as those who employ more than eight people. Overall, this group forms only 0.6 per cent of the population. The gap in their numbers between economically vibrant areas and backward areas is high, 3 per cent of it being in developed areas and 0.3 per cent in underdeveloped areas.[4]

These entrepreneurs initially emerged in the rural areas and in townships. Because of the ideological limitations of their position, this group was initially slow to expand. In the beginning they were largely made up of urban youth returning to the cities after the Cultural Revolution, laid

3. Li and Guangjin (2002): 118.

4. Ibid.

off workers and emerging rich peasants who had diversified into cash crops. They came from a low social background. After 1992, once the ideological limitation to their position ended, this group's social status rose and its economic clout increased. In the middle of the 1980s, as Zhang (2002: 54) points out, scholars were more interested in the 'internal composition, class nature and characteristics of this group'. Jia Ting and Wang Kaicheng (1989) pointed out that although they hired labour, they could not be characterised as capitalist exploiters because they did not live entirely on interest. Today, of course, China has very successful private entrepreneurs and this group has become the main group, able to rise socio-economically.[5]

4. Specialised technical personnel: This group consists of those involved in private joint ventures and state enterprises. They are an important group in China's drive towards modernisation and enjoy a high social status. They can also be seen as the modern intellectuals, as against traditional intellectuals.[6] However, they make up only 5.1 per cent of the total work force, of which up to 10-20 per cent is urban and an insignificant 1.5 to 3 per cent rural.

5. White collar or middle management workers: This section is made up of non-technical staff in all enterprises and adds up to 10-15 per cent of the total labour force.[7] This is also the one sector through which workers and peasants can improve their status and is the channel for upward social mobility. The number of these workers has increased since the reforms started.

6. Individual commercial and industrial workers: This section has also increased in number since the reforms and has been expanding since the 1980s. Since the 1990s, after the reform of state enterprises, a large population of erstwhile workers has entered this sector. This includes all kinds of services provided. They make up 4.2 per cent of the urban labour force.[8]

---

5. Interview Jia Ting and Wang Kaicheng, Beijing, September 25, 1989.
6. Li and Guangjin (2002): 119.
7. Ibid.
8. Li and Guangjin (2002): 120.

7. Commercial service sector workers: This sector is closely linked to the urbanisation process and consists of all types of commercial and service enterprises. In most urban areas they make up to 13-17 per cent of the working population and in rural areas, it is a mere 1.6 to 3 per cent. Thus, the rural-urban abyss is widening, especially since this is the sector, which is the growth engine in China—as it is in India.

8. Industrial workers: This group is largely marked by a decline in its social status both at the ideological and the income levels. Amongst the ordinary workers, again there is a marked difference amongst those working in the private sector and those still employed by the shrinking state sector. This difference translates into income, security and status. Zhang (2002: 52) points out how, during the reform of large and medium sized enterprises, about 30 million workers were made redundant—that is, 30 per cent of the total state labour force. Majority of them are women and middle-aged workers. This sector's share is 22.6 per cent of the total work force, of which 30 per cent are peasants.[9] This is because several younger workers in this sector have improved their technical skills and moved into other professions.

9. Peasants: This is the group that has undergone the most remarkable stratification. Today, there is abysmal gap between the rich peasant and the middle peasant, not to speak of the poor peasant, whose only escape is to leave every thing and go to the cities. The 'rich peasant' category can be further sub-divided into those engaged in fishery, animal husbandry and floriculture. The incomes of those involved in these commercial forms are much higher than those engaged in conventional farming. Li points out that the contribution being made to the national GDP by conventional farming has declined from 28.1 per cent in 1978 to 17.3 per cent in 1999.

10. Unemployed, laid-off workers and part time workers: These people are naturally hanging on to the lowest rung of the social strata. But, fortunately, according to Li they make up only 3.1 per cent of the total—a figure that is disputable if we keep in mind the way the manufacturing sector in China operates today. The *Blue Book of Sociology*, published by the Chinese Academy of Social Sciences (CASS) in listing these 10 groups

---

9. Li and Guangjin (2002): 121.

makes a clear and explicit distinction between each of the sectors and its members. The latest issue of the journal *Social Sciences in China* adds another group, i.e., intellectuals, to this list. Huang Ping divides intellectuals in modern China into three types: those inside the system, those outside the system and those opposed to the system. Those inside the system are the ones who help in policymaking, those outside are independent academic intellectuals and, finally, the objectors form the dissident groups (who have suffered for their stance). In this formulation, Wang Hui *et al.*, would come under the academic class.

Stratification in terms of income has been very interestingly dealt in an article by Sun Liping to examine this problem. Sun looks at the new methods through which resources were redistributed and at the process of the re-accumulation of resources. He points out that during the 1980s, this process was characterised by the emergence of what came to be known as *guandao* (bureaucratic profiteering). This helped a number of people possessing or having access to political and administrative power and become rich. Some of them became part of the *shi wan* (ten thousand households) and some went on to become well known entrepreneurs (Liping, 2002: 61). He points out that corruption and the use of government contacts remained a main source of wealth accumulation right through to the early 1990s and by the later decade of 1990s the sums involved were in millions of yuan. But then, in the 1990s, the losers in the reform process started to show up. This is all too visible in the income differences between the *noveau riche* and the marginalised poor.

Sun tells us that data showing the distribution of income of the various social strata forms a pyramid. According to him, a survey by a researcher in the People's University showed that the share of the total income received by the highest fifth of households was indeed high. In rural areas, the richest fifth of the households received as much as 48.9 per cent of the total, where as in urban areas it was slightly less, standing at 44.46 per cent. For the strata classified as intermediate, the household incomes were 15.01 per cent for rural and 15.77 per cent for urban households, that is, less than 20 per cent of the total.[10]

10. Ibid.: Liping (2002): 64.

Yiyong and Xin Xiaopai (2002) take a more detailed look at income differentials in China. The first major difference lies between the rural and urban areas. Giving statistics from 1998–2000, they show how rural incomes have been consistently lower.

Table 3.1

Income Differentials between the Rural and Urban Areas in China from 1998 to 2000

	Urban	*Rural*
1998	5458	2162
1999	5888	2210
2000	6316	2253
2005	—	—
2009	—	—

This data shows us that rural incomes are half that of urban incomes, although both are increasing. The paper also goes on to give us income differentials among the different professional occupations. It notes that jobs in the financial sector, electronics and information industries, aviation, tourism and insurance etc., have enjoyed the largest increase in incomes, in stark contrast to the traditional workers and peasants. It shows that incomes in capital and technology-driven industries have risen and those in labour intensive industries have fallen (Yang and Xin, 2002: 145). Differences among these different strata are also visible in terms of income, as is seen in Table 3.2.

Table 3.2

Differences among Different Strata Visible in terms of Income

Social Stratum	*Personal Income (monthly)*	*Family Income (monthly)*
Leader in institutions	2,000.0	3,500.0
Office workers	1,376.4	2,385.0
Professional and technical personnel	1,368.8	2,683.2
Commercial workers	447.7	2,720.1
Labourers	998.0	1,845.5

Source: Qiu (2002): 73.

Thus, in terms of income, there is a marked difference between different segments and allows us to clearly see the situation of the middle stratum. One also notes that most surveys concentrate on the different professional categories to specify social stratification. In this respect, the professional background of a person is likely to be the determining factor in terms of other forms of social and cultural capital.

This income differential is further corroborated by my research and also reveals the importance of 'occupation' in determining status and wealth. In Chengdu, for example, the average middle class salary is between 3,000-5,000 yuan and, to qualify as upper class, it has to be 10,000 yuan.

The Role of the Intermediate Strata or the Middle Class

The question that obviously arises is whether these different strata/ groups, (using the terminology the Chinese use) can at all be seen as classes, or whether interest groups will remain as they are, as also whether these groups actually have well articulated interests. A brief analysis of the data presented above and of the manner in which Chinese scholars are identifying separate interest groups makes it clear that, despite the small number that fall in the middle stratum, it is numerically significant, enough to be a powerful segment. However, in the main, this segment consists of the 'salaried' classes, with rich entrepreneurs forming the uncertain top.

Only one article could be found that deals directly with the emergence of this middle strata. This is by Xiaohong Zhou (2002); titled 'The Middle Class: Is it possible and is it necessary'. The article explores the rise of the middle class in China and attempts to theorise the issue. Using Marx, the author argues that the middle class is the inevitable result of industrialisation and in post industrial societies forms the majority.

As Zhou points out:

> Since the economic reforms of 1978, the class structure of Chinese society that had stabilised over the last thirty years again revealed a new change. One undeniable fact is the deepening and continuous impact Chinese economic reforms have made in changing China's social

> structure. Apart from the traditional working and peasant class, a new class has emerged,a new middle class stratum. This class, which had disappeared from the historical stage after the success of the Chinese communist revolution since 1949, has not only once again reappeared; it has developed with a remarkable speed.

A spokesman of the State Information Centre has commented: 'In the first five years after 2001, 200 million people will enter the middle stratum group'.[11] And the Deputy Chief of the Foreign Trade Bureau, in a speech in Singapore during the talks on China entering the WTO was even bolder. He predicted that, in 10 years, China would have 400-500 million people with middle level incomes.[12] However, there still remain certain ideological impediments. Official state documents warily avoid using the term 'middle class', by calling it 'middle income-stratum' or 'middle-income group'.

Zhou (2002: 8) goes on to define this group as those who belong to the following:

1. Post 1978 private entrepreneurs in cities and towns.
2. Post 1978 private shopkeepers and private manufacturers.
3. Government bureaucrats and intellectuals.
4. White collar employees in foreign companies.
5. Managers in different sectors; and
6. High income groups in new industries and students who have returned home from abroad and, finally, sports and media stars, models, and artists.

This division would also correspond with the first six categories listed by the *Blue Book of Sociology* (2002). Thus, we see that there is a definite segment in China, which corresponds to what is accepted as the middle class worldwide and it is increasingly being driven by consumerist hunger now pervasive in the better off section of Chinese society, be it for common commodities, luxury and leisure, or art and fashion. They are, to use Bourdieu's term, becoming 'distinctive in life style'. If one were to add up the percentages given by the *Blue Book of Sociology* in terms of the different strata, then the middle segment would form approximately 27.5

11. Zhou (2002).
12. Ibid.: Zhou (2002): 2.

per cent of the total working population. A pessimistic strain runs through almost all the writings on any positive role this stratum could play in the emerging civil society—and the reason they give for their cynicism is the continued and stifling control of the state and the CCP. As Qiu (2002: 79) points out,

> Although a market economy is necessary for a civil society, it does not necessarily lead to one. ...The unmatched and enormous role played by state power makes the people increasingly exert themselves to seek individual power. Under these circumstances, it is less possible for us to establish a civil society of equality and autonomy.

He goes on to say: 'We believe it is hardly possible for China to form a middle class with an independent social stratum of entrepreneurs and intellectuals as its main body'.[13]

Zhou (2002: 18) sees their main role in China as the frontline of consumers rather than a political force. This role, he says is already prominent. This consumerism has of course come under criticism and this class is dubbed as one 'which spends tomorrow's money to manage today'. He sees their political role as that of a rear guard. Zhou (2002: 16) puts it succinctly when he says:

> They are the group that has benefited the most since economic reforms, had access to better education and white collar jobs. At another level they have contributed to social stability. Essentially they draw their status from their salaries and jobs, and depend on themselves to further improve their status. ...Intellectuals and journalists from this segment have also tried to create public opinion in their favour. ...They want a stable society which allows them to maintain their positions.

It is these characteristics and the basic need for social stability that makes them the political rear guard. Thus, while the emergence of a middle class—for what it is worth—is self-evident, it certainly does not yet have what it takes to be called a civil society that can play a proactive role as an 'agent of change'. Instead, they have closely associated themselves with the goals of the ruling Party in the name of stability and to maintain the status quo.

---

13. Qiu (2002): 79.

Basic Problems of Social Stratification and the State's Policy Responses

The final point would be: the state/Party's responses to this emerging, dynamic and stratified society. China has undoubtedly made impressive economic gains over the last two decades and according to recent statistics managed to pull 220 million people out of poverty (Kuhn, 2004: 28). However, the miracle is marred by the increasing gap between rich and poor, both regional and within regions. Fan Gang points out 'how China has now entered a new and more painful stage of development, where the contradictions are clearly visible'. In a recent article published in the official *People's Daily*, he says:

> The development process of many countries shows that during this stage two development results may appear. In one scenario, a country successfully industrialises and modernises. In another, growing economic gaps and social tensions "cause development to stagnate, or even result in turmoil and regression".[14]

Today, China's leadership is painfully aware of the increasing social disparities and knows that if not addressed immediately, they could lead to large scale social instability in the near future. Already, reports of protests by laid-off workers, the spiralling incidence of crime and even reports of people dying of hunger are common (This was put at more than 90,000 last year). Apart from this, the poor record on work safety, the dying of miners, forcible land dispossession in the name of development followed by inadequate compensation, is beginning to hurt the image of the Party.

The government has responded by making a policy change in its earlier concentration on GDP growth. Today it is trying to initiate debate and discussion about slowing down economic growth, so that funds can be freed for social welfare programmes and redirected to re-erecting a collapsing rural health and education sector. It is also encouraging the emergence of NGOs and other civil groups that can locally tackle the problems faced by the poorer sections of society. There was a story in the local press of how an NGO had gone to court on behalf of migrant construction labourers who had not been paid wages for a year. The NGO won the case, a first of its kind. This, of course, would not have happened

---

14. People's Daily, 21 February 2004.

had the Party not supported the initiative. In fact, migrant labour is really the main problem in cities today and the state is making attempts to create more favourable conditions for them. This includes doing away with the household registration system, the main form of control. The state is also trying to put in place an objective legal system to address industrial and other disputes.

Further, it has also attempted to change the role of its frontal organisations, such as the All China Women's Federation, the Trade Unions and even the Youth Organisation and has turned them more into organisations that address the needs of newly emerging poor and laid-off workers by retraining them and by becoming employment agencies. The government's attempt to develop the Western region through infrastructure development and other forms of resource allocation is also one of the ways it is seeking to balance the growing regional imbalance. At the ideological level, the Hu and Wen team has tried to instill, with renewed vigour, the idea of 'social harmony' and the need to build a 'harmonious society'. This dream, along with the vision of a great and strong China, is seen as adequate compensation for hardship.

Conclusion

China is today a highly stratified society and this is visible on the ground and within the intellectual discourse in China. By giving a break down of the various types of education available and the disparities in the opportunities of access, this article attempts to provide a general overview of the new social reality in China—that of a highly stratified society and the role being played by education in further reinforcing this stratification. This is today's reality that will soon pose major problems for China. It is already fraught with serious ramifications where social stability is concerned, because it is creating, especially amongst the poor in urban and rural areas a large class of underpaid and undereducated people. Whether the Chinese government, through policies and better resource allocation, can remove these emerging inequalities remains to be seen. This, coupled with lack of social justice mechanisms inherent in a democracy, such as rule of law, trade unions, a free press and civil society action (i.e., such as that of NGOs as intervening agencies), means that those at the bottom of the pile are driven in to agitating against the state, then arrested, punished and victimised. China has allowed NGOs to intervene as a part of social development, but these are strictly controlled by the state and any questioning of policy or anti-state stance are strongly discouraged. To what extent China can balance the needs of specialised, highly educated manpower and its social policies of universal, quality education, is the challenge in this sector.

The picture of emerging social stratification in China presented in this paper is based primarily on Chinese sources on the subject. Western sources have been avoided deliberately, in order to ensure that the terrain for the enquiry is established in China itself. However it is easy to conclude that today's China no longer represents the egalitarian and strictly structured social system that it had earlier. Even if one were to look only at the different groups being identified by the Chinese sociologists, a deeper understanding of the social relations evolving within these groups gains great significance. Research carried out on the experience of East European socialist societies has also thrown light on the type of social changes that could come about in China. Kornai's (1995) whole work on this theme is exemplary. He has focussed on the way people's daily interactions changed due to the prevalence of what he calls, 'vertical dependency', where instead of depending on one's self, one relied on the state and its representatives to meet one's material needs. Today, in China this vertical dependency has certainly changed to one where one has to depend on oneself. Chinese society has evolved into a hybrid where vertical control continues to be exercised by the state Party apparatus, while survival and security becomes increasingly dependent on horizontal networking. In conclusion, China presents an excellent example of the complexity of social differentiation that is produced when a society undergoes economic and structural change.

References

Bian, Yanjie (1994a). *Work and Inequality in Urban China*. Albany State University: New York Press.

———. (1994b). "Guanxi and the Allocation of Urban Jobs in China", in *China Quarterly No.* 140: 971-98.

———. (1997). "Bringing Strong Ties Back in: Indirect Ties, Network Bridges and Job Searches in China", *American Sociological Review* 62: 366-85.

Bourdieu, P. (1987). *An Outline of a Theory of Practice*. Cambridge: Cambridge University Press.

Chongyi, Feng (2008). "Democrats within the Chinese Communist Party since 1989", *Journal of Contemporary China* 17 (57): 675. November.

Huang, Ping (1993). "Intellectuals Seeking a Destination While Drifting Aimlessly", *Zhonguo Shehui Kexue* 2.

Hui, Wang (2001). "Contemporary Chinese Thought and the Question of Modernity", in Xudong Zhang (ed.), *Whither China: Intellectual Politics in Contemporary China*. p. 161.

Ji, Zhou (2005). *Higher Education in China*. Thomson Learning Asia.

Jiang, Liu (ed.) (2002). *Blue Book of Chinese Society, 2002*. Beijing: Social Sciences Documentation Publishing House.

Kornai, Janos (1992). *The Socialist System: The Political Economy of Communism*. Princeton University Press.

———. (1995). *Highways and Byways, Studies on Reform and Post-Communist Transition*. Cambridge: MIT Press.

Kuhn, Anthony, (2004). "The Death of Growth at Any Cost", in *Far Eastern Economic Review*, April. pp. 28-31.

Li, Chunling (2002). "The Class Strucutre of China's Urban Society during Transition", in *Social Sciences in China*, Spring. pp. 91-99.

Li, Chunling and Chen Guangjin (2002). "Report on the Social Stratum and Structural Changes", in *Blue Book of Chinese Society*. Beijing: Social Science Publishing house. pp. 115-132.

Li, Lulu (1999). "On Social Stratification", *Shehuixue Yanjiu* 3.

Li, Peilin (1995a). "Structure of Classes and Strata and the Changes in Interest Structure in the New Era", *Zhongguo Shehui kexue* 3.

———. (1995b). *Report on Classes and Strata in the New Era in China*. Liaoning Peoples Publishing house.

———. (2002). "Introduction: Changes in Social Stratification since the Reform", *Social Sciences in China*, Spring. pp. 43-47.

Li, Qiang (2002). "New Changes in Social Stratification", in *Blue Book of Chinese Society*. Beijing: Social Sciences Document Publishing House. pp. 133-143.

———. (2001). "Conflicting Occupational Prestige Evaluations in the Transitional Period in China", *Social Sciences in China*, Spring.

Liping, Qiu (2002). "A Study and Discussion of Social Strata in Chinese Cities Today—Taking Shanghai as an Example", in *Social Sciences in China*, Spring. pp. 69-80.

Liping, Sun (1996). "Relations, Social Relations and Social Structure", *Shehuixue yanjiu* 5.

———. (2002). "Re-accumulation of Resources: The Back-ground of Social Stratification in China in the 1990s", *Social Sciences in China Today*, Spring. p.21-39.

Liu, Xin (2002). "Strata Consciousness in Transformation-era Urban China", in *Social Sciences in China*, Spring. pp. 81-89.

Riskin, C. (1987). *China's Political Economy: The Quest for Development since 1949*. Oxford: Oxford University Press.

Ruan, Danqing *et al.* (1997). "On the Changing Structure of Social Networks in Urban China", *Social Networks* 19: 75-90.

Sato, Hiroshi and Keiya Eto (2008). "The Changing Structure of Communist Party Membership in Urban China, 1988-2002", *Journal of Contemporary China* 17(57): 654. Routledge.

Stockman, N. (2000). *Understanding Chinese Society*. Oxford: Polity Press.

Thakur, Ravni (2000). "The Reform of the Hukou Zhidu: A Comment", *China Report* 36.

The Blue Book of Sociology (2002). Beijing: Social Sciences Document Publishing House.

Yang, Yiyong and Xin Xiaobai (2002). "Status and Trends in Income Distribution", in *Blue Book of Chinese Society, 2002*. Beijing: Social Sciences Document Publishing House. pp. 144-164.

Yu, Heping (ed.) (2002). *Zhongguo gongmin shehui de xingqi yu zhili de bianyan*. Beijing: CASS.

Yun, Kangpan (1989). *Shehui xuezhi dui Shehui de jinggao* (Warnings about society from sociologists). Beijing: Chinese Women's Publishing House.

Zhang, Wanli (2002). "Twenty Years of Research on Stratified Social Structure in Contemporary China", *Social Sciences in China*, Spring.

Zhang, Xudong (2001). *Whither China: Intellectual Politics in Contemporary China*. Duke University Press. p. 2.

Zhongguo shehui kexue yuan (1994). *The Project Group of Chinese Private Entrepreneurs*, "Operation of the Chinese Private Enterprises and the Group Characteristics of Private Enterperneurs", in *Zhongguo Shehui kexue* 4: 60-76.

Zhou, Xiaohong (2002). *Zhongchan Jieji: Heyi keneng yu Heyi ke wei?* (The Middle class, is it possible and is it necessary?, Sociological Seminar No. 15, September 18, Department of Sociology, Nanjing University.

4 China's Handling of the Process of Globalisation

C.V. Ranganathan

For a country to ably handle the process of globalisation to its benefit, it needs to gear up domestically in a variety of ways, so as to take advantage of the international availability of capital, technology, market access, human, and material resources and easy communications. A country so enabled will learn to understand and rely on global market conditions and to create interdependence with its chosen partners. China is an outstanding example of a country that has managed the whole process admirably well to achieve a very impressive economic growth. It has lifted tens of millions of its vast population to unprecedented levels of well being, at the same time firmly sticking to mono Party rule for over 50 years—all this by deftly adapting to the changing requirements in its growth trajectory.

Deng Xiaoping, who succeeded Mao Zedong as the supreme leader of China after the latter's death, initiated economic reforms in 1978. He had then told a foreign statesman that he and his colleagues were at first just 'groping the stones to cross the stream,' meaning that the Chinese leadership was carefully taking things step by step, as there was then no single blueprint for the reforms or any models to follow. Despite all that, the cumulative effect of the reforms initiated on an experimental basis—before the measures were formally adopted—were such that it became the country's path to progress for the next two decades and, when globalisation came, China was one of the few countries which was ready to take up the challenge and take advantage of the phenomenon. Deng Xiaoping may never have dreamt of globalisation, but he ushered a politically and economically isolated China into a globalising world by creating the necessary conditions within the country.

This success story is well recorded in scores of academic works: China as the factory of the world having perfected mass production in a wide range of consumer goods in high demand; China as one of the largest consumers of resources from fossil fuels to grain to airplanes to military hardware; China as a huge destination for investments; China as a country with huge export surpluses; and as a country whose economic growth and military prowess had brought it influence and prestige. Its departure from the foreign policy adopted during Mao's rule resulted in reconciliation with erstwhile enemies, so that China and its neighbourhood became a large area of relative peace.

Dengist economic reforms were paralleled by ideological moves that freed thinking from its Maoist straight jacket. The Mao saying, 'Practice is the sole criterion of truth' was turned on its head. Ideology, unlike in Mao's time, became inductive and a means of validating empirical realities. This showed finesse in the ability to use ideology to suit policy decisions made on a pragmatic—not ideological—basis.

One systemic achievement of Deng was to get the Mao veterans to take a backseat and to induct younger Party members into positions of authority. Although Deng may have been responsible for firing at least two of his *protégés* from high office, he placed a premium on higher education, field experience and expertise as criteria for the selection of cadres to high office, rather than the candidates' longevity in the Communist Party of China (CCP).

Nearly a decade and a half after Deng set the foundations of a China gearing up for globalisation, there came the collapse of the former Soviet Union and all the Communist governments in Eastern Europe. Deng's answer to this phenomenon was to stake his personal prestige, during the last years of his life, by giving a further push to economic reforms, validating their correctness and staving off opposition to his moves from the Party's leftist's conservatives. At the same time, one of the four cardinal principles underlying reforms, the dominance of rule by the CCP, was strongly reiterated. A very lengthy and thoroughgoing study was initiated at high levels of the Party to study the reasons for the collapse of Socialist Parties everywhere and some major conclusions were drawn from them for China. One definite conclusion reached was that the CCP could not survive as the dominant ruling Party unless it could deliver better living standards for the masses, both rural and urban. This involved both economics and the ushering in of gradual changes in the politics of governance. The Communist Party of Soviet Union collapsed because it had become stagnant, rigid, ossified and disconnected from reality. Gorbachev committed the heresy of abandoning Marxism and weakening the foundation of the Leninist Party structure in initiating '*perestroika*' and imitating models of Western socialist democracies. The Chinese, however, were quick to take advantage of his foreign policy, particularly of the overtures he made for reconciliation with China. Curiously enough, these internal studies praised Khruschev for his leadership qualities while, not surprisingly, dismissing the Indian model as unsuitable for China. The principal purpose of these studies, apart from drawing some negative lessons, was to focus on how the CCP should adapt itself to the growth of China's economy, which was accompanied by rising expectations among the masses for fairer, non-arbitrary governance, greater sensitivity to grievances, and a more accountable, transparent and a corruption-nepotism free ruling Party elite.

The Tiananmen Square incident in 1989 was not really a protest for strengthening democratic institutions, as commonly believed. It was overwhelmingly motivated by the expectations referred to above, as personally witnessed by this author. Following the episode, when conservative senior Party officials and 'elders' prevailed in sacking Zhao Ziyang, the Party Secretary who made a show of sympathy with the demonstrators at the Square, the reform process was slowed down. There followed international condemnation of the use of disproportionate force to deal with demonstrators, boycotts and reduced flow of investments and inter-governmental aid. Deng's response, after a hiatus of three years, was (as mentioned above), to give a powerful push to economic reforms. More important, the Chinese Foreign Office worked energetically on the diplomatic front to vastly improve China's relations with the erstwhile Soviet Union, Vietnam (with which China fought a war in 1979), Indonesia and Singapore (with which diplomatic relations at Ambassadorial levels were resumed) and with the

Association of South East Nations (ASEAN) to get out of the diplomatic isolation imposed by the West.

The shortlived economic boycott by the West was lifted when it became clear that China was back on the course of economic reforms and that foreign investments on preferential terms were now welcomed.

Also, there was hope of China opening wide its domestic markets in various manufacturing and service areas as a precondition for entry into the World Trade Organization (WTO), negotiations for which had been started. The negotiations lasted a long time, involving bilateral and multilateral forums and, finally, China's admission came in 2001. Judging by the final outcome, China made far reaching concessions and commitments with respect to market openings, acceptance of standards, willingness to abide by legal procedures laid down and to negotiate in good faith within WTO Jiang Zemin, who became General Secretary of CCP in 1989 and later President of China, attached priority to what was described as 'great power diplomacy'. He saw the WTO membership as an essential ingredient of this policy and it was important for China to resume a more normalised relation with USA, European Union and Japan after the break in 1989. The second term of President Clinton saw a vast improvement of relations between China and USA, with high-level exchange of visits and new items being brought on the political agenda, including non-proliferation of nuclear weapons. The Jiang-Clinton summit meetings helped bury Tiananmen Square memories and gave China the equality of status with the US as a great power. All this marched impressively alongside the double digit growth of GDP. But it needs to be pointed out here that the major portion of Jiang's tenure as state, Party and military head coincided with strong emphasis on social stability and growth at any cost, with little regard for equitability or the aberrations that had crept into the Party, eroding its credibility. In an attempt to regain credibility in the people's eyes, the Party launched a campaign under Jiang's supervision who enunciated what was called 'The Important Thoughts of Three Represents'. He declared that the CCP would henceforth represent: the advanced productive forces in society; advanced modern culture; and the interests of the vast majority of the people. This move, not popular or welcomed at the time, signified a radical departure from what was laid down 80 years earlier, to the effect that workers, peasants and proletariat were the vanguard of the Party.

Zheng Bijian, Vice-Principal of the Party School and a policy adviser, in a private conversation said that the thoughts grew out of CCP's assessment of the reasons for the Soviet Union's collapse and a three-year long assessment of the CCP's weaknesses. The Party was now required to adapt to meet three developments: globalisation and the advance of science and technology; diversification of Chinese society and societal institutions and lifestyles; and lax Party organisation and the need to improve the quality of the rank and file of the Party. The thoughts also grew out of lengthy debates on the scope of marketisation and state-owned enterprises. They challenged the three major elements of socialism: planned economy, the dominance of public ownership and the distributional principle of 'to each according to his work' and sought to replace these with new approaches sanctioning fuller marketisation, greater role in the national economy for private ownership and wider circulation of assets (Shambaugh, 2008).

While the 'theory of three represents' was proclaimed in 2001, and was followed up with propaganda within and outside the Party circles, there were no noticeable moves for admission on the part of the growing entrepreneurial groups till much later. The probable reason was the existence of a cozy relationship that had come into being between local governments, private businesses and local Party officials. Thus, the opening up of the Party to private entrepreneurs and intellectuals, the targets of the first category mentioned above, was not availed of in a hurry. Recruitment to the Party from this sector only picked up later in 2005.

It could be said that by the end of the tenure of Jiang Zemin as state and Party head, decisive steps had been taken on the external political front to strengthen China's quest for international economic integration through maximising the advantages of globalising its economy. However there were huge social problems in pursuing the 'growth at any cost' model caused by an alarming gap in social stratification, as also by his apparent preferential treatment for coastal regions and major cities. In 2002, when the Hu Jintao-Wen Jiabao combination took over as Party head and premier, there came a major shift in policies, resulting in increasing incidents of social unrest involving tens of thousands of people in the hinterland and interior regions.

In a continuum from 2002 Hu Jintao and Wen Jiabao launched a series of ideological campaigns to confront the multiple problems in the wake of growth and rising prosperity. At the same time, major institutional reforms were brought in to make the Party a better instrument to oversee the implementation of Hu and Wen's ideas. Briefly, the policy agenda from 2002 shifted towards three components which have proven popular within and outside the Party as also in the country at large. These are: more balanced regional economic development; increased concern for social justice and social harmony; and greater transparency in the functioning of the Party and state machinery, combined with stronger institutionalisation in political governance and internal security.

On the ideological side, Hu Jintao supplemented his predecessor's vision of building a 'well-off society' which would ultimately lead to a 'harmonious, socialist society'. Such a society, according to Hu, should feature democracy, the rule of law, fairness, justice, stability, orderliness and harmony between mankind and nature. The enunciation of such a vision reflected the enormous social and other problems and sought to combine positive elements rooted in traditional Confucian concepts and contemporary socialist precepts for solving these problems.

These ideas were developed further in 2004-05. Hu enunciated the 'scientific development concept'. This attempted to propound a remarkably comprehensive policy blueprint spread over multiple topics. These included: improving the rural situation; overcoming energy bottlenecks and more efficient use of resources; fostering innovation and competitiveness; reforming the administration system; improving transparency in government; transforming the functioning of state-owned enterprises without allowing asset stripping; controlling pollution and environmental degradation; improving public health and safety; solving the internal migration problem; constructing new social security systems; improving relations with ethnic minorities; and top to bottom improvement of the Party apparatus.

In 2007, Premier Wen Jiabao wrote an article for the *People's Daily* aimed to address the heated internal debates on democracy. The salient points he made were that China must follow its own path in building democratic politics and that the socialist system and democratic politics are not mutually exclusive. He called for perfecting the legal system as an important hallmark of a mature socialist system. The emphasis on the exclusivity of the Chinese path to socialist democracy was a rejection of other models of democracy.

Complementing these broadly announced ideological goals was the adoption of the Eleventh Five-Year programme (2006-2010) by the National People's Congress (NPC), whose main objectives were meant to alleviate problems of social stratification and rising levels of inequality through building 'a new socialist countryside'. Among the objectives of this programme were: doubling the 2000 GDP per capita of 7,086 Yuan by 2010; developing a number of major enterprises into internationally competitive companies with well known brands; improving the income levels and the quality of life for urban and rural residents; consolidating the nine-year compulsory education system; developing a sound social security system; improving environmental conditions; improving legal institutions, introducing a national employment policy; and pension insurance coverage.

Taken cumulatively, these objectives represent a big shift from previous policies and are certainly more humanistic. At the same time, the security apparatus has been strengthened a great deal to respond to riots and disturbances, controls over the use of internet to politically challenge the regime have been tightened and harsh measures used to deal with violent protests in places such as Xinjiang and Tibet.

A comprehensive attempt to reform the CCP's organisation and its ruling capability were made with the adoption of 'the decision on the enhancement of the Party's governing capacity' at the 16th Party Central Committee Plenum in 2005. The thrust of the decision was to strengthen Party committees at all levels, increase Party members' awareness of the renewed ideological imperatives outlined above, improve inner Party democracy and combat corruption and laxity within the Party. The decision was followed up by an intrusive, Mao style rectification campaign—interrogating members and exposing them to criticism and self-criticism. Practically all the 70 odd million Party members were involved in this campaign and it lasted over different phases for 18 months. Fighting corruption and improving Party discipline were other important requirements. The Central Discipline Inspection Commission (CDIC) and the Ministry of Supervision were merged. For rebuilding the local Party apparatus, a very important requirement to enhance the Party's capability and credibility, emphasis was laid on holding elections for Party committee heads, establishing committees among the newly emergent social and professional groups, improving extra-Party consultations and supervision of Party's functioning by non-Party persons.

As the Hu-Wen regime sees it, increasing inner Party democracy is the key to the spread of democratic norms in the country at large and for this, various means, such as adoption of multiple candidates for grassroots election of local Party committees and opening all committees to intra-Party criticism was encouraged. Improving cadre competence is sought to be achieved by mid-career training and strengthening vetting and approval process by the CCP Organisational Department at all levels for the appointment and promotion of cadres at all ranks. The Soviet-style nomenclature system for higher level cadres and the *'bianzhi'* system for government level appointments through competitive exams or nominations is to be refined. The ideological rectification campaign referred to above weeded out 45,000 cadres as unfit and identified many others as weak and vulnerable.

A crucial component of the institutional strengthening of the Party is the Party school system. Directly linked to the service background of Hu Jintao, there are reportedly some 2,700 Party schools all over China. Every one of the 73 million strong Party is expected to study in these schools. Broadly, the curriculum in these schools includes study of major Party policy documents, administration, management and leadership, economics and current affairs, international relations, accountancy, Party history, etc. The Central Party School at Beijing, of which Hu was the head, has emerged as a leading think tank in China. It has opened its doors to training personnel outside the Party, including army men, businessmen and others.

Lastly, with Hu Jintao and Wen Jiabao coming to power, it can be said that transitions of leadership have become less opaque and factional interests are mediated through intense discussions before formalisation at Party and state conclaves.

Also, the two prospective leaders who will take over in 2012 and 2013 (when the constitutional term of the present duo ends) have been tentatively chosen and given greater responsibilities so that they can familiarise themselves with the tasks awaiting them in the highest office. Since the turn of the century, a common feature in the Central Committee of the Party and of the State Council (government) is that their membership is composed of well educated technocrats, who have served in various capacities at lower provincial and district levels.

China's impressive growth over the decades is well known, but what the above account shows is that, at least from the early years of this century, China has attempted to refashion national objectives and the available governing instruments in order to keep up with the times, with of course, the CCP remaining the centre of power. It also shows an increased sensitivity and a stronger response to the multiple problems facing China in the social scene, where millions had been excluded from the growth process; even before the global crisis, the current leadership had launched ambitious plans for the uplift of these millions. Universally perceived as having succeeded broadly in managing the first phase of the globalisation process (pre-2008), it now remains to be seen how China manages the huge negative impact on it of the second phase (post 2008). A refocus on pressing domestic issues was no doubt the need of the hour for China, but its external dependence did contribute to its growth in a large measure. It is this dependence that will not be restored for some time to come, but the present crisis does give China an opportunity to prepare for again creating new domestic conditions that would be needed when global economic growth bounces back to normalcy.

References

Shambaugh, David (2008). *China's Communist Party-Atrophy and Adaptation*. Woodrow Wilson Center Press.

5 Ways of Thinking

Psycholinguistic Reflections on Sino-Indian Relationships and Potentialities

Ravi Bhoothalingam

The emergence of India and China as global leaders to be of the 21st century has drawn worldwide attention. Eminent journals have speculated on a scenario in which the two nations would overtake the USA in GNP terms—China by 2030 and India by 2050. The US National Intelligence Committee has gone to the extent of examining the military implications of China's rise and its consequences for world geopolitics. Many academic treatises have addressed the theme, predicting all manner of outcomes ranging from peaceful collaboration, to war. Not to be left behind, popular magazines and newspapers took up the India-China theme, liberally using the term 'Chindia', coined by Indian Minister of Environment, Jairam Ramesh. Meanwhile, the western media has picturesquely played up the perceived dichotomies between the two civilisations by depicting China as a dragon (in Western terms, menacing) and India as an elephant (wise but lumbering), quite ignoring the meaning of these symbols in their respective cultures.

My avid interest in China started well before all this, an interest intensified by 15 years of travel and exploration all over the country. I have no claim to being a scholar or an economist, but often during my travels I pondered over the differences between India and China. Could there exist, I wondered, identifiable ways of thinking that are distinctive to the Indian and Chinese psyches, and if so, what might the implications reveal? Could they throw light on some frequently asked questions like: What explains the Chinese prowess in infrastructure and manufacturing? Will China ever become a democracy? Will China and India be friends?

On a more practical note, reading Ranganathan and Khanna's (2004) excellent work reminded me that the 1962 Sino-Indian conflict arose out of a disastrous 'chain of misperceptions and misunderstandings'. Going by recent events, this situation seems ominously likely to arise again, as neither of the countries appear, in the meantime, to have even tried seriously to gain a deeper knowledge about and understanding of the other, let alone read each others' signals. But, going to the positive side, what opportunities does mutual engagement open for the two countries? And what would the simultaneous rise of these two nations mean for the world?

Despite growing trade ties between India and China—total trade by 2008 was nearly US $52 billion, growing at 50 per cent annually[1]—the two countries are yet to engage with each other in a meaningful way, either on the economic front, or indeed, in any other area. Investment flows are weak, tourism a mere blip. Until 2007, the only direct flight between Beijing and Delhi was still by Ethiopian Airlines—a service started four decades ago! Even this much-hyped trade growth is heavily dependent (nearly 75 per cent) on low-value primary products out of India, while the trade deficit with China is growing. Meanwhile, the rest of the world rushes to exploit the strengths of China as the 'world's factory' and increasingly of advanced technology and R&D. Japan, Korea, Vietnam and Taiwan, are all heavily involved in China. Each still has serious political issues with China, some with long and bitter histories, but these have not held them back from vigorous engagement with a rapidly growing Chinese economy, all for mutual benefit.

But, according to the global consultants, McKinsey & Co.,[2] whilst 25 per cent of executives worldwide regard China as their most important growth centre after the USA, only 4 per cent of Indian CEOs share that belief. Similarly, only 2 per cent of Chinese bosses see India as a major growth point. Despite the formidable reputation of Indian as well as Chinese businessmen for seeking out profit anywhere in the world, they seem wary of treading into each other's country. Both

1. Annual trade and growth figures for the years 2004-2008. *General Administration of Customs of the People's Republic of China Annual Statistics.*
2. Survey cited in the McKinsey Quarterly, March 2005.

governments are cautious—India's much more so. Amongst the citizenry on both sides, a yawning knowledge gap prevails. Whilst active in all other directions, India and China remain *terra incognita* to each other.

This lack of mutual awareness is no longer just an academic weakness. I believe it can be a serious impediment to India's growth, blinding us to opportunities. Importantly, it even constitutes a vulnerability that leads to conflict. To paraphrase *Sunzi* (ancient military treatise), 'foreknowledge of the other'—friend or foe—is vital for any kind of policy formulation. But where does one start? Most accounts that try to 'explain' China or India rely on economic or political analyses. But might there not be a more basic factor? After all, both politics and economics are driven by human agency, and what distinguishes humans from animals is the development and use of language and the influence of culture. Can language and culture reveal both the potentialities and the pitfalls of the India-China engagement? This paper searches for possible answers.

A Psycholinguistic Model

Pursuing this train of thought led me to the following simple model, which goes:

- Language influences thought and perception.
- Perception guides behaviour.
- Collective behaviour creates a culture.
- Culture creates special competences; and
- Competences influence economic development.

I shall focus here only on the relationships between language and thought (the latter word being used interchangeably with perception), and then between culture and development.

Language and Thought

Language is what differentiates man from animal. Whilst many species communicate with each other, only man has developed language, the ability to learn it and then hard-wire it in his brain. The interrelationship between human thought/perception and language has been the subject of much debate in psychology. Early thinkers such as Benjamin Whorf and Edward Sapir[3] thought of language as being somewhat like a pair of tram-lines along which thought and perception ran without any deviation, bound by the rules of that particular language. Others like Chomsky (1993) and Pinker believed that thought was intrinsic to human existence, with a 'universal grammar' serving as a common tool of human expression, regardless of whichever language was spoken. Both sides in this debate adduced much evidence from anthropological observations of peoples belonging to different cultures.

Current psycholinguistic thinking, drawing on the latest neuropsychological research on how the brain processes thought into language, converges broadly on what is known as the 'modified Sapir-Whorf hypothesis' (Boroditsky, 2003). This holds that there is a highly interactive feedback loop between thought and its expression—i.e., language—and whilst linguistic rules may not be quite the rigid 'tramlines' as earlier contemplated, the unique characteristics of each language will specify inclinations that predispose thought and perception (e.g., of time and space) in a certain direction. It is rather like loading different operating systems on to a computer. Microsoft or Apple software will all perform the normal functions—e-mail, presentations, photography etc., but each system has its own strengths which make some operations easier, others more problematic. An even better analogy is water running down a hillside—the deepest and steepest channels will carry the most water, though others will have some flow as well, and water can even be forced uphill through the application of sufficient energy. The more dissimilar the languages, the greater will their respective speakers vary in their thinking patterns.

Chinese and Sanskrit

Whilst both India and China have a range of languages, the Chinese character script has been common across that country for over two millennia, mediating communication between, say, Mandarin and

3. Bloom (1981).

Cantonese speakers, and thus has played a powerful unifying role in China. India has a greater diversity of languages, but a broad linguistic and cultural base of Sanskrit underlies the majority of these languages. Accordingly, it would be a reasonable first approximation to consider Mandarin and Sanskrit as the root languages of the two civilisations and examine what their differences might imply. With this proviso, let us examine the case of Sanskrit and Mandarin as the root languages of the Indic and Sinic civilisations respectively, and consider the implications of language structure on ways of thinking.

The ideographic and monosyllabic Chinese language has preserved a remarkable continuity through the centuries. Each Chinese character is understood in the same way all over China, though local languages may pronounce the word differently. This unity of language across time and space has been very powerful as a unifying force, conferring living history and shared identity. One sees this daily in the allusions to classical phrases, poems and history, and in the prevalence of proverbs that pepper everyday speech. The Chinese language has no singular or plural, no tenses, moods or cases. Yet, because of its ideographic nature, each character has great specificity of meaning, which is comprehended as a whole pattern in itself. The abundance of different words for the same concrete things can be quite striking: for example, several words describe the adjective 'old' depending on whether one refers to a person over 60 years of age, or over 70, etc. The word for 'contradiction' is '*mao-tun*' or 'sword/shield'. Mandarin describes things by specification, often based on imagery or analogy, rather than analysis. It has been suggested that the discipline involved in learning to write Chinese characters, (starting from the age of three), with each character written following set rules and with a particular order of strokes, has been instrumental in the meticulous and orderly approach—i.e., there is a way of doing things—that the Chinese bring to manufacturing.

As earlier mentioned, language shapes the way one thinks and vice-versa; this is now well established in the science of linguistics. Hajime Nakamura (1964), (the eminent Japanese Indologist and Sinologist, whose book *Ways of Thinking of the Eastern Peoples* inspires the title of this essay) believes that the Chinese bent of mind for understanding phenomena through direct perception is a consequence of the concrete and visual nature of the Chinese script. Indeed, modern neurological research reveals that deciphering the ideographic Chinese script is akin to a pattern-recognition mechanism of the brain. The Chinese character patterns stimulate the right side of the brain, especially the parietal and occipital lobes where such processing takes place. Since speech functions are localised on the brain's left, Chinese thus promotes a more holistic utilisation of the brain. The great scientist and inventor of calculus, Leibniz, was so struck by the power and economy of Chinese that he remarked: 'If God were to give man a language, that language would be Chinese!'

On the other hand, metaphysical speculation and the elaborate logic built on language were far more developed in India. Sanskrit as an alphabetic language could not be more different in structure and grammar than Chinese. Nakamura establishes how Sanskrit deals more efficiently with concepts that involve change or transformation than does Chinese. Sanskrit lends itself to expressing ideas of great complexity through its simple principle of word agglomeration, for example from '*nari*' to '*ardhanari*' to '*ardhanarisvara*' etc. Further, in Sanskrit, the addition of prefixes and suffixes can continue almost without end, and the resulting megacompound-word/sentence can be split up once again in multiple ways. These exercises introduce interesting complexities and ambiguities in meaning, which can be generated by anyone with time on their hands and gifted with a certain skillful playfulness in manipulating the language. Sanskrit grammarians and poets were adept at such feats: for example, poetry that reads front to back as well as vice-versa. Similar capabilities have been recognised in the work done by Indian software geniuses today.[4]

Similarly, in Sanskrit, any noun or adjective can become an abstract noun by adding '*ta*' or '*tva*.' Together with the general use of the passive voice and the use of positive-negative combinations ('*laabhaalabhau jayaajayau*'), Sanskrit thus encouraged abstract and universal thinking, grammar and complex analysis. Not that the Chinese were not capable of complexity, but they were more adept at expressing it through a pictorial

---

4. Lecture by Prof. Leslie Young (2007). Hong Kong University, to CII CEO delegation, June 2, at the Cheung Kong Business School, Beijing.

idiom. Patterns enable strong expressions of paradox and contradiction. One of the best instances of this is the explanation of the 'I Ching' in hexagrams—powerful in its very simplicity, without any loss of meaning.

Given the unitary nature of Chinese characters and the power of their pattern recognition mode, it is not surprising that in China, great attention was paid to historical records, precedents and maintenance of annals. In India on the other hand, the development of a strong tradition of oral history and recitational poetry meant considerable interplay between history, imagination and mythology. Chinese role models are drawn from history. Indian role models are mainly mythological figures. The China-India comparison has many examples of the literal juxtaposed with the metaphoric. Take this story about Confucius. When he was asked by a pupil: 'Master, tell us the meaning of death?' his rather curt reply was: 'How can we understand death when we still do not understand life?' Contrast this with the story of Nachiketa and Yama in the Katha Upanishad when Nachiketa confronts the Lord of Death with the question: 'What happens at the moment of death?' leading Yama thereupon to deliver an elaborate exposition on the nature of the 'Absolute'.

Chinese Culture and Confucius

In the incessant comparison between India and China, the sheer visual evidence of China's public infrastructure—roads, airports and bridges—stands out. Yet, giant infrastructure projects are nothing new for China. The Great Wall, the Grand Canal linking the Yellow River and the Yangtze, and the gargantuan 2,000-year old irrigation works of Dujiangyan among many others, are all part of ancient Chinese history. These were not monuments built to glorify any individual ruler, but are truly part of classically defined infrastructure—public investments for the larger common good. What motivated the then emperors to labour over these works for decades, each building on the efforts of his predecessor? Did the people willingly participate in these endeavours, or were these projects the fruits of slave labour exacted under imperial coercion?

Perhaps the Confucian ethic still has a role to play. Although Mao Zedong tried his best to denounce Confucius and eradicate his teachings, even he had to admire the Confucian ethic for its emphasis on public education and social order. The heritage of 2,500 years does not die easily, says Bell (2007). What Confucius says in his *Da Xue* ('Great Learning') still sounds strikingly scientific and contemporary, and a model of inductive reasoning from the first principles:

> When things are investigated, knowledge is extended, When knowledge is extended, thoughts are made sincere, When thoughts are made sincere, the heart and mind are rectified, When the heart and mind are rectified, the personal life is cultivated, When the personal life is cultivated, then the family is regulated, When the family is regulated, the state will be in order, When the state is in order, there will be peace throughout the world.

Notice that Confucius does not theorise about the meaning of freedom or justice. Confucianism strongly emphasised the network of obligations, duties and relationships that bind an individual to the family, community, state and society. Individual ethics and social order were harmonised: 'Maintain harmony though difference exists' is a famous maxim. Right action is not only the correct moral course for a person: it also makes the state-community a better entity. The Chinese propensity to align individual goals and actions to larger social and national objectives and create mass mobilisation of people, (without giving much thought to individual freedom) owes much to the Confucian legacy, and cannot be ascribed only to coercion or state diktat.

Following the inductive logic aptly illustrated by the *Da Xue*, this Confucian legacy—ingrained deeply in the Chinese psyche—emphasises the importance of moving step by step from the specific to the general, from the small to the large. The Chinese state is faithful to this precept, encouraging local units to innovate and experiment. When successful, local results are scaled up to a national level; if not, the unfortunate local Party functionary is consigned to a post deep in the interior. Far from being a top-down process, Chinese experimentation follows the time-honoured proverb of 'crossing the river by feeling the stones'.

But this is not the only tradition from which the state draws inspiration. There is a strong current of the legalist philosophy underlying the realpolitik,—a coercive apparatus and brittleness that mark China's governance methods. The complex nature of challenges to come will put these methods to the test. But both Legalists and Confucians would agree on one thing—Confucius's prescription to a king on how best to rule his people: 'Enrich them! Teach them!' succinctly expressing motivations towards wealth and education shared by politicians and people alike. Here, perhaps, lies the thought that can transform Sino-Indian relations.

India and Gandhi

In India, our experience of diversity in daily life, whether of caste, creed, language or custom, has generated a flair for flexibility and cultural adaptation that is widely recognised, not the least in the adaptability of Indians to new environments. The Indian mind also seems capable of operating at several levels, simultaneously holding views that may be directly in opposition. I am reminded of my experience as a child, going for an *'idli'* breakfast at the house of astronomer and physicist Dr. K.S. Krishnan, FRS After his *'puja'*, he meticulously rendered astrological advice to his family early every morning, but come 8 o'clock, was dressed in his suit and ready to leave for his office at the National Physical Laboratory, where he replied to letters from Einstein and Eddington. Indians take this kind of rare 'twobrain' ability for granted. The Chinese are constantly amazed at our fluency with languages and grasp of other cultures, our ability to deliver results amidst apparent chaos, and our flexibility in coping with issues both mundane and serious.

Gandhi personified the complex Indian mix of contradictions, and uniquely brought out its genius. He was deeply spiritual, yet thoroughly open-minded, and certainly not narrowly religious. He was morally upright to a degree many thought quixotic, yet he had a wicked sense of humour and fun. Gandhi was rooted in the soil of India and could thus innovate a novel form of protest, *'satyagraha'*, which immediately caught the imagination of the poor and illiterate masses of India but, at the same time, confused and confounded the British rulers. An Empire was defeated with very little blood being shed. Gandhi focussed on serving those most oppressed by India's caste system, concentrating on unglamorous but essential features like abolishing untouchability and promoting sanitation and hygiene. The similarity between Confucius and Gandhi is striking, with their initial focus on specific individual action, continuing in ever-widening circles to embrace the entire universe.

The distinctive modes of thinking in the two countries also give a clue to their failures. India has had problems in establishing both the structure and pattern of governance across large swathes of its national territory. In China's case, structural rigidity in its governance procedures has caused the emotional alienation of its outlying provinces. India has not generated mass mobilisation of opinion in favour of rapid progress in health, education and infrastructure. In China, overenthusiastic or coercive mass mobilisation by the bureaucracy has resulted in much harm and injustice to its people.

Distinctive Competences: China and India

The discussion so far about the specific qualities of Chinese and Sanskrit as also of the two cultures leads one to infer that there should be distinctly separate spheres in which the Indians and the Chinese should display their distinct and statistically comparable capabilities. When the then Chinese Prime Minister Zhu Rongji visited India in 2003, he proposed (in a practical spirit worthy of Gandhi and Confucius) cooperation in information technology, with India being the lead partner in software and China in hardware. This is a common idiom today, yet China still looks up to India's software industry with admiration and not a little envy. But we can also look further afield for potential synergies. What about India's design skills being married to Chinese manufacturing techniques? China's advances in biology, immunology and genetics can be tied in with Indian skills in health care delivery and nursing, both of which now command a world market. Consider pharmaceuticals. Theory would assert that China should lead in structural chemistry whilst India would dominate combinatorial chemistry, both areas being vital elements for making new drugs. This hypothesis is indeed borne out by the actions of the world's large pharmaceutical companies in their investment activities in the two countries (Business Week, 2006).

Could India's prolific and highly creative film industry partner with China's flawless choreography and production values? Imagine films like 'Asoka' set in India or Central Asia, drawing on the magical themes surrounding the Silk Route! Consider the attraction to audiences in China of a new *Journey to the West* or *Crouching Tiger, Hidden Dragon* shot in India with extravagant Bollywood music and dance, and what it would do for tourism to India. What about corporate alliances between India's management-cum-consulting skills with the Chinese organisational ability to execute gigantic infrastructure projects? Would Chinese student and youth tours to India be more popular if combined with a summer programme in English language or IT? What about India's English and multilingual abilities allied to Chinese pedagogical methods? The list of such complementary abilities can go on.

Creativity and Innovation in India and China

In the areas of creativity, innovation and research, the differences in Chinese and Indian approach exhibit an array of complementary competences. As would be predicted from our psycholinguistic model, Chinese innovations arise largely from trying to view problems (patterns) from unusual angles, to use inversion and analogy, and thereby generate novel solutions that might initially appear contradictory or paradoxical. The example of creativity in drug discovery, given earlier, is a case in point. So are a number of 'break-through innovations' listed by Prof. Ming Zeng (2007) in his recent research, as well as advances in architecture and railway engineering. The 'one country, two systems' formula for the resolution of the Hong Kong issue is itself an early and striking example of such thinking. But it is revealing that the Dalai Lama's 'Middle Path' formula to resolve the Tibetan question finds little resonance in China; one reason might be that this formula by its very nature suggests an incremental, continuing process whose end-point is neither as predictable nor as amenable to control as a known alternative pattern, novel as that might be.

The Indian approach to innovation revolves around the ability to handle and harness chaos and complexity with ease—even to find pleasure—in dealing with and manipulating probability and uncertainty.

This is best seen in, but not limited to, India's success with software. But at another and more popular level, India's distinctive innovatory competence can be best summed up in the oft used word *'jugaad'* (loosely meaning improvisation)—a concept familiar to travellers on Indian roads on vehicles prone to several types of mishap. For every such risk of a breakdown, a ready solution is available even in the most remote areas in the shape of improvised repairs and low-cost substitutions. Whilst these are by no means permanent solutions, they enable a quick and inexpensive continuation of the journey. This spirit of generating speedy solutions through local materials and very low-cost substitutions has most recently been demonstrated on an industrial scale in the 'Nano' small car. Carlos Ghosn of Nissan-Renault has announced that a rival to the Nano would be designed entirely in India through collaboration with Bajaj Auto. Similar experiments elsewhere in India aim at low-cost computers and cell phones.

A Pax Sino-Indica and its Potential for the World

To summarise, the Chinese way of thinking emphasises the pragmatic and the concrete with great visual imagery and a strong sense of civilisational history, geography and unity. Its ethical legacy values orderliness and harmony, *albeit* to an oppressive extent. In India, a vibrant, loosely held, imaginative and creative collection of people has strengths of complex and abstract thinking, along with flexibility in dealing with multiplicity, diversity and uncertainty. These two sets of attributes seem incompatible. Yet, like yin and yang, the combination of these two baskets of skills is exactly what is required in the conduct of business in today's world. Imagination without order would be chaos; structure without vibrancy would be sterile. A relationship that judiciously utilises the strengths of both the nations could trigger off a number of outcomes beneficial to the region and the world. The specific steps that India could take are specified below.

First, focus on developing and demonstrating its economic competences on a global scale. This will evoke greater respect for India in China, as also in Asia, Africa and Latin America. Second, keep the border issues on the back burner, focussing instead on building a deep and growing economic relationship with China based on complementary strengths. This is the best bet for overcoming the prevailing uneasy bilateral climate of suspicion. The examples of China's relationship with Japan, Korea, Vietnam and, most strikingly, Taiwan have shown that comprehensive economic engagement—comprising trade, tourism and investment—creates an extensive and expanding community with mutual interests that can over-ride even the most primeval of historical animosities and political differences. Remember: 'enrich them! teach them!' If the prospects for public prosperity and popular education loom bright, war cries will disappear, or else remain at the level of rhetoric.

Finally, it is not difficult to imagine the power of an 'innovation engine' that couples the Chinese and Indian approaches to innovation as described earlier. Consider bi-national teams working with both inductive and deductive logical models, using radical pattern-change methods along with probabilistic and chaos theory, or combining low-cost substitutions with economies of scale. Even in their approaches to handling contradictions, the two cultures differ. Brought together, these diverse skills could generate a mass of new ideas and convert them into production volumes required by large populations. In both countries, problems of poverty, deprivation, ill health and inequality cry out for such solutions. Such a partnership should not limit itself to bilateral matters, but go on to address pressing global issues such as climate change, a new financial and security architecture as well as a new moral order for the planet.

These problems require radical thinking and novel solutions, both of which could be the offspring of a marriage of Indian and Chinese ways of thinking. Issues of such dimensions are appropriate challenges for two ancient civilisations that seek to reinvent themselves as modern states and potential superpowers. Farsighted political leadership should set their sights in this direction and create the conditions to move speedily towards these goals. Diplomacy, in the final analysis, lies in comprehending the world-views of both the dragon and the elephant and then employing the necessary sequence of communication and levers of influence and incentives. The two creatures are very different indeed, but they live in the same, single ecological entity—the world. Remember that *long-xiang* (dragon elephant) was the Chinese translation of the

Buddhist protective deity naga (Chung, 2008). This suggests, once again, a central place for language and psychology in bringing about Sino-Indian synergy. I would like to believe that both Sunzi and Chanakya would concur.

References

Bell, Daniel (2007). *China's New Confucianism: Politics and Everyday Life in a Changing Society*. Princeton University Press.

Bloom, Alfred (1981). *The Linguistic Shaping of Thought*. Psychology Press.

Boroditsky, L. (2003). "Linguistic Relativity", in L. Nadel (ed.), *Encyclopaedia of Cognitive Science*. London: MacMillan.

Business Week (2006). *Novartis in China: East meets West in R&D*. November 6.

Chomsky, N. (1993). *Principles and Parameters Theory in Syntax: An International Handbook of Contemporary Research*. Berlin: de Gruyter.

Chung, Tan (2008). *Rise of the Asian Giants: Dragon-Elephant Tango*, edited by Patrica Uberoi. Delhi: Anthem Press.

Nakamura, Hajime (1964). *Ways of Thinking of Eastern Peoples: India, China, Tibet, Japan*. Rev. English trans. (ed.) by Philip P. Wiener. Honolulu: East-West Center Press.

Ranganathan, C.V. and Vinod C. Khanna (2004). *India and China: The Way Ahead*. Har-anand Publications.

Zeng, Ming (2007). *Dragons at Your Door: How Chinese Cost Innovation is Disrupting Global Competition*. Harvard Business School Press.

Acknowledgements

I thank Dr. Stephen Hicks, Department of Clinical Neurology, University of Oxford, for reading this essay carefully and for his expert comments on brain function and neuro-anatomy. Any remaining errors are solely my responsibility.